QUESTIONS AND ANSWERS
ON COMMUNISM

Questions and Answers

on

COMMUNISM

Richard Cardinal Cushing

Third Printing

ST. PAUL EDITIONS

Published by the DAUGHTERS OF ST. PAUL
Jamaica Plain, Boston 30, *Mass.*

FOREWORD

This booklet on Questions and Answers concerning Communism has been published with the hope that it might serve to arouse many from a state of apathy and indifference towards an international conspiracy that is bent on the domination of the world.

The questions are those most frequently asked in classrooms and lecture halls. The answers are taken mainly from Communist writings.

Papal encyclicals, reports of Congressional Committees and other sources of information, facts and guidance are quoted to substantiate our evaluation of the true and subtle nature of the enemy that confronts us.

This booklet, however, is by no means the complete picture of Communism nor a full answer to it. Whereas many would not read one or more of the innumerable volumes already written on the subject, they might study a summary of this type.

If they will, I pray that it may prompt them to live the way of life that is spelled out in the Gospels and the Ten Commandments. That way of life, for individuals and nations, is the first and greatest answer to the Communist peril. Thereafter every good reform needed in our country will follow and the roots of Communism in our midst will be destroyed.

†Richard Cardinal Cushing

TABLE OF CONTENTS

CHAPTER I

COMMUNISM, MARXISM, SOCIALISM

1. QUESTION: **What does Communism mean?**

   ANSWER: A. Literally it means the common ownership of all material goods: No private, individual ownership of wealth, property or productive goods.

   B. It is based on a world view called "dialectical materialism," which seeks to interpret the world as coming into being without God and to prove that He does not exist.

2. QUESTION: **How does Communism contend that it will "prove" that God does not exist?**

   ANSWER: A. By the assertion (which is only an assertion and which can readily be refuted) that matter is auto-dynamic or self-creating and

   B. By the promise (which is only a promise) of bringing about an earthly paradise, the so-called "Communist society."

3. QUESTION: **What will be the conditions of this "Communist society," according to the Communists?**

   ANSWER: It will be an era, they contend, where there will be no State, no family, and no morality of any sort. Man will be able in this condition, they foolishly assert, to end all unhappiness, neurosis, and ill health. Also, in that "Communist society," there will be "lasting peace" and "for the first time, genuine freedom."

4. QUESTION: **Are there any supposed stages in this achievement of the "Communist society?"**

ANSWER: Yes, the first stage is supposedly the achievement and consolidation of the world Soviet dictatorship or world socialism, which must be brought about in each country first by guile and then by violence. After this dictatorship has become world wide, the Communists contend it will actually "wither away" and in its place will come the promised earthly paradise or the Communist society.

5. QUESTION: **Have the Communists ever been able to answer the five proofs of St. Thomas Aquinas for the existence of God?**

ANSWER: No, they have always evaded the teachings of St. Thomas Aquinas.

6. QUESTION: **Is there actually any system of Communism anywhere?**

ANSWER: No. The word is a popular fraud. In Russia and in the other countries subject to Soviet rule, the leaders of the State control all wealth, property, and industry. They also, by that very fact, control the utterances and expressions of everyone, dominating every agency of public information.

7. QUESTION: **What does Communism (or its alleged current stage of socialism) actually mean?**

ANSWER: It means that all power, political, economic, social, and financial resides in the State, namely in the hands of the Soviet rulers.

8. QUESTION: **What is the proper name for this system?**

   ANSWER: Marxism or Soviet Fascism, which means that all power is in the control of a few persons. It is extreme socialism which deifies Matter and the State. In its philosophy, the clod becomes God and man becomes a slave.

9. QUESTION: **What is Marxism?**

   ANSWER: It is an alleged political-economic system (based on this world view of dialectical materialism or the denial of God) named after its founder, Karl Marx, born in Germany in 1818, died in England in 1883. He renounced both Judaism and Christianity in turn and became an avowed atheist. His principal works are **Das Kapital** and the **Communist Manifesto,** both written in collaboration with Frederick Engels.

10. QUESTION: **What was the background of Frederick Engels?**

    ANSWER: Engels, who was born in 1820 and died in 1895, was the son of a wealthy textile manufacturer who had mills both in Germany and England. Engels not only wrote some of the most important Marxist works but also contributed financially to Marx' support.

11. QUESTION: **What is the theme or message of the two chief Marxist works?**

    ANSWER: A. **Das Kapital,** called the bible of Marxism, the first volume of which was completed in 1867, is a long, complicated treatise in three volumes on the history of the class struggle through the ages, allegedly culminated in class warfare between the workers and their oppressors, namely the capitalists or the employing class. It contains the philosophy of Marx (Dialectic Materialism), his economic theories, and his proposed methods of removing most economic and social evils.

B. **The Communist Manifesto,** 1848, outlines the strategy for all workers of the world in overthrowing the hated system of Capitalism: to take wealth and industry from the middle and upper classes (Bourgeoisie) and allegedly transfer them to the workers, i.e., the Proletariat. (Actually, by standing for "the dictatorship of the proletariat," which is in reality the dictatorship over the proletariat, Marx and his successors prevented or tried to prevent that wider diffusion of property which is essential to social progress and justice.)

12. QUESTION: **Did Marx and Engels write other books besides these two chief ones?**

ANSWER: Yes, they produced a great number of works, from **The Holy Family,** written before the **Communist Manifesto** all the way over to **Ludwig Feuerbach** and the **Dialectics of Nature,** written by Frederick Engels after Marx' death. Each one of these books seeks to denounce the existence of God and the value of religion as the basis for all Marxist teachings.

13. QUESTION: **Why is the basic teaching of Marx called Dialectical Materialism?**

ANSWER: A. Materialism denies the existence of any non-material reality such as God, the

soul, and the world of the spirit. "The
only reality is matter" is a constant Communist refrain. Marx used the scientific
fact that the matter of the universe is in
constant motion, often evolving into new
forms of mineral, plant, and organic life
to prove that this also applies to the basic
creation of life and the origin of the human mind. How life and reason ever developed from atoms and molecules of
mere matter Marx does not and cannot
explain. Nor can he tell us how the motion which he makes so much of can
come into existence without a First
Mover, namely, Almighty God.

B. The Dialectic according to Marx is the
logic or "method" of his theory of materialism. It supposedly rules the inevitable
laws of nature, society, and right thinking. It is based on the false assumption
that every idea (and every development
in nature and history) contains within itself its opposite or denial. This is called
the operation of Thesis, Anti-thesis, and
Synthesis. For instance, in our present
period of history, the Communists contend that the thesis (or ruling class or
"thing that is") is the so-called bourgeoisie; the antithesis is the proletariat; and
the synthesis is the dictatorship of the
proletariat or socialism, the first stage of
Communism.

Actually, we have seen that this alleged
dictatorship of the proletariat is nothing
other than the dictatorship of the Com-

munist Party. This fact is acknowledged by both Lenin and Stalin, the latter in his famous **Problems of Leninism.**

14. QUESTION: **What is the name given by the Communists to the alleged operation of the "laws" of dialectical materialism in society?**

ANSWER: It is called by the Communists "historical materialism," which Frederick Engels claims is one of the great "discoveries" of Karl Marx.

15. QUESTION: **What are some of the errors in the theories of Karl Marx?**

ANSWER: A. His false basic assertion that God does not exist and that the universe has come into being without God. From this all the other errors of Marxism flow.

B. His equally false statement that history is entirely determined by economic factors. As with all errors that try to win man's acceptance, this is partially true. But the great religious, judicial, and other "idealistic" developments in world history did not arise from economic influences. It could be shown that even Marx' own teaching begins as something which arises from the process of thought, that is, not the outcome of material or economic forces.

C. Marx and Engels regarded private ownership of property as essentially evil. It is the abuse or misuse of private property which is evil. What the Marxist view of private property will finally lead to in the destruction of the family is testified to by Engels in his famous work, **The Origin of the Family, Private Property, and the State.**

D. The labor involved in producing any material commodity is not the principal factor in its value, as Marx claimed. Skill, demand and supply, climate, weather, etc., are important factors of value.

16. QUESTION: **What are some important truths in the writings of Marx?**

ANSWER: A. The fact that millions of workers in Europe, England, America and elsewhere were underpaid, or unemployed.

B. The fact that Economic Liberalism (irresponsible use of capital) was a common cause of this condition.

C. The deplorable conditions of child-labor in the 19th century.

Note: Marx failed to realize that Socialism would lead, as it has, to worse exploitation of the workers than the system of Private Enterprise. Marxism-Leninism as a whole, in attacking the undoubted abuses of "monopoly" in the capitalist system, could only offer as their solution a still greater monopoly in dictatorship of a Party and hence of a very few through the State apparatus. This led to the monopoly not only of property but also of the press, all other avenues of information, and hence, the control of thinking.

17. QUESTION: **Why is Marxism today called "Marxism-Leninism" by the Communists?**

ANSWER: Because the teachings of Marx and Engels were later supplemented by those of V. I.

Lenin, who re-affirmed strongly the basic materialism of Marxism and in addition the necessity under the Marxist theory for the final violent overthrow of all non-socialist governments. This necessity, he averred, applied also to the governments of the United States and Great Britain, which must "inevitably" be overthrown by violence in order to introduce socialism.

As Joseph V. Stalin puts it in his **Foundations of Leninism:** Leninism is Marxism of the era "of the proletarian revolution". To which he adds: "To be more exact, Leninism is the theory and tactics of the proletarian revolution in general, the theory and tactics of the dictatorship of the proletariat in particular."

18. QUESTION: **What are the "Marxist-Leninist classics" to which the Communists always refer in their writings?**

ANSWER: They are the teachings and therefore the works of "the great scientists of Marxism-Leninism," namely, Karl Marx, Frederick Engels, V. I. Lenin, Joseph V. Stalin, Mao Tse-tung, and today Nikita Khrushchev.

19. QUESTION: **Does the Catholic Church condemn Socialism in theory and practice?**

ANSWER: Several recent popes, especially Leo XIII and Pius XI, have frequently stated that Socialism in any form is wrong. Strict Socialism puts all productive goods under the ownership and control of the State contrary to the individual right of ownership. The control of Education, and of every other social institution, is a natural consequence. What is popularly called "Limited Socialism," such as State or Federal control of Railroads or Communications, may be necessary in the interest of the common good. However, "the Limited Socialist experiments" in England, for example, have done little to improve social and economic conditions.

20. QUESTION: **What three things should be borne constantly in mind in connection with Soviet Communism?**

ANSWER: These three things are:

A. The nature of Communism, flowing from its world outlook of dialectical materialism and therefore the "necessity" of setting up the world Soviet dictatorship first by guile and then by violence, in order to usher in the "earthly paradise" of the Communist society.

B. The nature of the Communist line and the methods by which it is introduced by infiltration into every non-Socialist country. The Communist line is that series of proposals which Moscow initiates and then wants the so-called "free world" to adopt in order to bring about the weakening of non-Socialist countries so that they may be eventually destroyed.

C. The true Communist attitude toward reforms. By this we will know that reforms are used by the Communists merely as a "screen or cover" for their illegal activities to bring about the dictatorship. This is what Stalin tells us in his section on "Revolutionism and Reformism" in his **Foundations of Leninism.**

REFERENCES AND SUGGESTED READINGS:

1. Budenz, Louis F. **Men Without Faces.** New York: Harper and Brothers.
2. Budenz, Louis F. **Techniques of Communism.** Chicago: Henry Regnery.
3. R. N. Carew Hunt. **Theory and Practice of Communism.** New York: Macmillan.
4. Gitlow, Benjamin. **The Whole of Their Lives.** New York: Scribner and Co.
5. Hoover, J. Edgar. **Masters of Deceit.** New York: Henry Holt and Co.
6. Kravchenko, Victor. **I Chose Freedom.** New York: Scribner and Co.
7. The Rev. Charles A. McFadden. **Philosophy of Communism.** New York: Benziger Brothers.
8. Pius XI. **Encyclical on Atheistic Communism,** March 19, 1937.
9. Sheen, Bishop Fulton J. **Communism and the Conscience of the West.** Bobbs and Merrill, Pub.

CHAPTER II

THE NATURE OF COMMUNISM

1. QUESTION: **What does Pope Pius XI declare to be the first or basic cause for the rapid spread of Communism?**

   ANSWER: In the middle of his Encyclical, **Divini Redemptoris,** (on Atheistic Communism) Pope Pius XI asks the question: "How is it possible that such a system, long since rejected scientifically and now proved erroneous by experience, how is it, We ask, that such a system could spread so rapidly in all parts of the world?"

   And he answers: "The explanation lies in the fact that too few have been able to grasp the nature of Communism."

2. QUESTION: **What, then, is the nature of Communism?**

   ANSWER: As we have seen, Communism is not so much a social or economic theory, as most people suppose, although certain outstanding social and economic theories flow from its original premise. It is rather a world outlook, an alleged explanation of how the world began automatically and how it will "inevitably" go forward in the history of man.

3. QUESTION: **Is there strong proof in the Marxist-Leninist "classics" and in the continuing Communist**

comments on them that dialectical materialism is the world outlook of the Communists?

ANSWER: Most decidedly. This conception saturates all
the "classics" and for Marx and Engels is
summed up in Engels' noteworthy work,
Ludwig Feuerbach. This work, completed
in 1888, not only seeks to summarize and
pronounce "dialectical materialism" as the
world outlook of the Communists, but seeks
to go on to show that this viewpoint does
not permit the least thought of any "reality"
but matter. It is stark, naked materialism.
V. I. Lenin continued and expanded on the
emphasis of dialectical materialism as the
Communist world view in the whole of
volume XI of his **Selected Works.** Stalin
summed up the whole assertion when he
wrote: "Dialectical materialism is the world
outlook of the Marxist-Leninist party. It is
called dialectical materialism because its ap-
proach to the phenomena of nature, its
method of studying and apprehending them,
is **dialectical,** while its interpretation of the
phenomena of nature, its conception of these
phenomena, its theory, is **materialistic.**"

4. QUESTION: **Do the Communists consider this affirmation
of this world outlook to be important?**

ANSWER: They have considered this basic thought of
so much importance that they have reprinted the statements by all "the great Marxist
scientists" in this regard over and over
again, in many different forms. It is the trag-
edy of America and most Americans, including many of our leaders, that this huge
distribution of Marxist-Leninist fundamental

literature goes on without their knowing anything about it.

As an illustration, chapter no. 4 of his **History of the Communist Party of the Soviet Union,** in which Stalin makes his statement on dialectical materialism and then explains it at length, is distributed by the thousands of copies as a pamphlet entitled **Dialectical and Historical Materialism.**

5. QUESTION: **Has any recent Communist declaration re-asserted this basic foundation of dialectical materialism?**

ANSWER: The Program of the Communist International, adopted by the Sixth World Communist Congress in Moscow in 1928, sums up its beliefs by beginning with the phrase: "Advocating and propagating the dialectical materialism of Marx and Engels and employing it as a revolutionary method of conceiving reality..." From thence it goes on through the entire range of resulting Communist beliefs to the logical declaration that it (the Communist International) "openly comes out as the organizer of the International Proletarian Revolution."

The famous Declaration of Communist and Workers Parties of Socialist Countries, issued in Moscow in November, 1957, asserts: "The theory of Marxism-Leninism derives from dialectical materialism. This world outlook reflects the universal law of development of nature, society and human thinking. It is valid for the past, the present and the future."

6. QUESTION: **Do we have additional proof in the writings of Communist scholars that dialectical ma-**

terialism is the all-embracing world outlook upon which all their other views are based?

ANSWER: Yes, we have it in the writings of every Communist theoretician. As an illustration, Maurice Cornforth, the British Communist scholar, in his work, **Materialism and the Dialectic Method,** says definitely that the theory on which the Communist Party establishes all its theories and policies "is the theory of Marxism-Leninism." Then he says: "And it is not just an economic theory, not yet exclusively a political theory, but a world outlook—a philosophy."

7. QUESTION: **How do the "laws" of dialectical material-ism operate in nature, according to the Communists?**

ANSWER: Matter and motion have always been inseparable, they contend. This motion, producing different stages in the development of nature and mankind, is always a motion of conflict or debate, dialectical motion.

8. QUESTION: **What is the fundamental and devastating weakness of this theory right in the beginning?**

ANSWER: Its weakness is—and from this it never recovers—that neither Marx nor Engels nor any of their followers can explain from where this alleged motion comes. They cannot answer the argument of St. Thomas Aquinas that the existence of motion in matter proves the existence of the First Mover, Almighty God. Engels admits that the Communists do not know the origin of this alleged motion, expressing the hope that in time science will be able to show how it develops.

9. QUESTION: **Despite this flimsy and false foundation, how do the Communists proceed to explain the workings of dialectical materialism in nature?**

ANSWER: Their contention is that the motion in what we consider to be inert matter (the original matter of the world) caused that which was at that time (thesis) to be challenged by the new form of life that was to be (anti-thesis) and out of this conflict came a new stage (synthesis). In this way, in these first stages, there developed life, then after millions of years, higher forms of animal existence, then after more millions of years there came into being man himself.

10. QUESTION: **Do the Communists try to present in detail the course of this dialectical conflict or motion in nature?**

ANSWER: Yes. They assert that in the course of this motion or struggle, there first begins to develop what they call a **quantitative** change, which after a time brings about a great and violent leap. Through that process, there comes about a **qualitative** change, namely, a new stage in nature.

11. QUESTION: **What are the five arguments for the existence of God given by St. Thomas Aquinas which the Communists evade in this alleged theory of dialectical materialism?**

ANSWER: The five arguments for the existence of God, which the Communists cannot answer are:
a) The existence of motion in matter proves

the existence of a First Mover, moved by no other, and that is God.

b) In the world of sensible things, there is an order of efficient causes, but there is no cause known which is found to be an efficient cause in itself. Therefore, it is necessary to admit a first efficient cause, God.

c) In nature, everything that we observe has a possibility to be and not to be, becoming generated and then corrupted. This makes it necessary for a force which has an existence of its own, called God.

d) There is a gradation to be found in things regarding their goodness and the like. There must be therefore something which is to all beings, the cause of their being, goodness and every other perfection. That is God.

e) The design existing in the universe, whereby natural bodies which lack knowledge nevertheless act for an end, indicates that there is some intelligent being by whom all natural things are directed. That is God.

12. QUESTION: **Is the dialectical materialism of the Communists, then, any different from the mechanistic materialism of the 18th Century?**

ANSWER: No, since the Communists are unable to prove whence their alleged motion comes, they are in no better way than the old materialists who found themselves in difficulty because they could not show how mankind or the world could come into being without God.

The alleged "law of opposites," whereby the Communists contend that every existing thing or being has within it a "unity of opposites," which sets it into motion, is totally unproved.

13. QUESTION: **Nevertheless, Marxism-Leninism goes on, does it not, to assert that this dialectic motion also exists in society through what is known as historical materialism?**

ANSWER: That is correct. It asserts that accordingly there was originally primitive Communism, then the slave state, then feudalism, capitalism, and inevitably after that, socialism, or the dictatorship of the proletariat.

14. QUESTION: **Is there a fundamental defect in this interpretation of history?**

ANSWER: There are many defects, which we shall have to examine later. One of these is that the claims that economic conditions determine the morals, religion, and law of each period is not true. The Catholic Church has existed through the slave state, feudalism, and capitalism.

Another defect of this theory is that it cannot account for periods of retrogression in history.

15. QUESTION: **How is it, according to the Communists, that the world Soviet dictatorship will "wither away" into the perfect Communist society and thus end the dialectical process in history?**

ANSWER: They base this theory on a false understanding of the nature of the state, as we shall see when we come to that subject. But they assert that this earthly paradise will come about as though it were an unanswerable truth. At the 21st Congress of the Communist Party of the Soviet Union, Nikita Khrushchev even announced that the beginnings of this Communist society will open up in Soviet Russia and the captive nations at the end of the next seven years.

16. QUESTION: **According to Marxism-Leninism, what is necessary to bring in this earthly paradise of the Communist society?**

ANSWER: It is necessary that the Soviet dictatorship, or socialism, shall become world-wide—established, maintained, and consolidated on a world scale. Or, at least, that the capitalist (or free) world shall become so encircled and weakened that the world-wide character of the dictatorship will be assured.

Then, the dictatorship will supposedly wither away of its own volition, yielding its place to the Communist society without state, law, family, morality, church. At the same time, it will supposedly end all unhappiness and ill health.

17. QUESTION: **What practical problem does this determination of the Communists to build the world Soviet dictatorship, in order to bring about the earthly paradise, present to the United States and the other free nations of the world?**

ANSWER: It presents them with the cold, hard fact that they cannot deal with Soviet Russia or with the international Communist conspiracy by way of negotiations, without bringing about defeat of the free world. The Communists will use every method—negotiations, civil war, as in the Baltic countries, Korean wars, and thrusts against us as in the Middle East and Asia—in order to obtain the world Soviet dictatorship.

18. QUESTION: **Does the record of Soviet Russia regarding treaties bear out this conclusion?**

ANSWER: Yes. Studies of the Senate Sub-Committee on Internal Security of the United States show that Soviet Russia has broken fifty of the fifty-two treaties it has signed.

REFERENCES AND SUGGESTED READINGS:

1. Special study is suggested of **The Philosophy of Communism,** by the Reverend Charles J. McFadden, OSA.
2. **Basic Writings of St. Thomas Aquinas,** edited by Anton G. Pegis. Vol. I., Random House, New York.
   (A brief critical analysis of some of the Communist writings referred to in this and other chapters will be found at the end of this booklet.)

CHAPTER III

CLASS WAR AND
THE COMMUNIST LINE

1. QUESTION: **According to Marxism-Leninism, what is the dynamic force which brings about the dialectical motion in society—the carrying forward of thesis, antithesis, and synthesis?**

   ANSWER: It is the class war, sometimes also called the class struggle. Marx and Engels stressed this idea definitely in the **Communist Manifesto,** when they said: "The whole history of mankind ... has been a history of class struggles, conflicts between exploiting and exploited, ruling and oppressed classes."

2. QUESTION: **Did Pope Pius XI also warn us of the class war theory of the Communists?**

   ANSWER: Yes. In the noted Encyclical on Atheistic Communism, His Holiness refers to the "trickery" of the Communists, giving as one example the following: "Thus, aware of the universal desire for peace, the leaders of Communism pretend to be the most zealous promoters and propagandists in the movement for world amity. Yet, at the same time, they stir up a class warfare which causes rivers of blood to flow."

   Then the Pope added: "And realizing that their system offers no internal guarantee of peace, they have recourse to unlimited armaments."

3. QUESTION: **Did the Communist Manifesto develop this idea of the class war to make it a universal phenomenon of all history?**

   ANSWER: It did. And so we read: "The history of all hitherto existing society is the history of class struggles. Freeman and slave, patrician and plebian, lord and serf, guild-master and journeyman, in a word, oppressor and oppressed stood in constant opposition to one another, carried on an uninterrupted now hidden, now open fight, a fight that each time ended, either in a revolutionary reconstitution of society at large, or in the common ruin of the contending classes."

4. QUESTION: **Is this theory of the class war based on valid grounds in history?**

   ANSWER: No. Like practically all Marxist concepts, it is an over-simplification of the facts, a fitting of the facts into a preconceived idea.

5. QUESTION: **In what way is the Marxian theory of the class war an over-simplification?**

   ANSWER: In countless ways. Historians and philosophers have pointed out that this theory, making all history the result of a dialectical process inevitably followed through and operating solely by means of economic motives, pressures, and conflicts, fails to take into consideration a thousand cross-currents that characterize history.

6. QUESTION: **This false theory of the class struggle is bound up, then, in the idea of economic determinism in history?**

   ANSWER: Yes. The basic idea of Marx (since there are no actual spiritual forces except those that arise from materialistic conditions) is that the driving force of the class struggle comes from economic conflict. That idea, in turn, is taken from the false conception that all religion, law, and other spiritual developments of an epoch in history are actually the outcome of the mode of production and distribution of food, clothing, and shelter.

7. QUESTION: **Does the history of Communism itself disprove this materialistic conception of history?**

ANSWER: It emphatically does. Christopher Dawson has pointed out in his **Essays in Order** that Marxism-Leninism had its origin in the mind of "that arch-individualist, Karl Marx, and the forces that inspired him were neither of the economic or of the material order."

8. QUESTION: **Do we see this theory of the class war disproved in our own day?**

ANSWER: Of course we do. The alleged victory for the working class in Soviet Russia and in other Soviet-controlled countries is actually a victory for the dictatorship of the Communist Party, itself under control of an oligarchy ruled by one dictator. The present personal dictator of the whole Soviet domain is Nikita Khrushchev.

9. QUESTION: **In addition, wherein again does this theory of the class war carried by means of the dialectical method prove to be false?**

ANSWER: In the static character which is given to it in the future. The dialectical process, represented in history by the conflict of classes, is supposed to come to a complete halt when the world Soviet dictatorship has ushered in the Communist society or earthly paradise.

10. QUESTION: **Is the theory of the class war, although false, of serious concern to us today?**

ANSWER: It decidedly is; for the Communists contend that this "class war" has now developed into the international arena. It is being fought out primarily between the greatest "bourgeois" state, the United States of America, and the "camp of socialism, peace, and democracy," Soviet Russia. As we shall see later, under the Marxist ethic or Leninist morality, the Communists will use any means, fair or foul, to bring about the destruction of the United States in this "class war."

11. QUESTION: **In the present "class war," do the Communists hold that there must be violence at every step of the Red techniques in defeating the enemy?**

ANSWER: No, although the final achievement of the "dictatorship of the proletariat," which is the consummation of the "class war," must come about through violence.

12. QUESTION: **This means, does it not, that the historical and successful carrying forward of the "class war" in the United States must result in the violent overthrow of our government?**

ANSWER: That is correct. Stalin put it well for the Communists in his guide book, **The Foundations of Leninism,** when he wrote: "The dictatorship of the proletariat cannot arise as the result of the peaceful development of bourgeois society and of bourgeois democracy; it can arise only as the result of the smashing of the bourgeois state machine, the bourgeois army, the bourgeois bureaucratic machine, the bourgeois police."

13. QUESTION: **Does this violent "smashing" of the governmental machine apply to the United States?**

ANSWER: Yes. It emphatically applies to the government of the United States which from the Communist viewpoint must be overthrown by violence. Both Lenin in **State and Revolution** and Stalin in **The Foundations of Leninism** have stated specifically that the Government of the United States must be overthrown by violence, in order to achieve the Communist goal of the "proletarian dictatorship."

14. QUESTION: **But it has been said that every step in the class war is not necessarily to be pursued by violence?**

ANSWER: Of course not. The Communists must first undermine the governments of "bourgeois" states by getting them to follow the Communist line and thus persuade them to undermine their own strength.

15. QUESTION: **What is the Communist line?**

ANSWER: The Communist line is that series of proposals which Moscow wants free world countries to adopt at any particular period in order that those countries will weaken themselves by thus doing what Moscow wants them to do.

16. QUESTION: **How is the Communist line carried forward in any particular non-Soviet country?**

ANSWER: As Stalin has so clearly set down in his **Foundations of Leninism,** the Communist

Party in each country is to forward the Communist line by means of non-Communists and "non-party organizations," making of them "transmission belts" for this Communist line.

17. QUESTION: **The Communist line is often carried forward in any particular country, then, by non-Communists?**

ANSWER: Yes, that is its particular strength. Concealed Communists, following the directives given by Moscow, whether in Government, press, television, or anywhere else, pursuade leading non-Communists of the value of the line.

18. QUESTION: **Has the line been prevalent in decisions in the United States, in the attitude of our Government, the press, and the like?**

ANSWER: It has been the secret of Soviet success in the United States, persuading first our press and our other sources of information in large part, to spread it through America, and then getting certain leading officials in the Government to follow Moscow's directives.

19. QUESTION: **Has this been an effective method to influence the United States to help build up Soviet Power throughout the world?**

ANSWER: It has been the decisive means by which Moscow has induced the United States during the past twenty-five years—sometimes with hesitation, but always too frequently— to build up Soviet Power. It can be said that none of the nations now behind the Iron Curtain (known as captive nations) would be enslaved by the Soviet dictator-

ship today were it not for the aid given
that dictatorship by our Government and
our sources of information.

20. QUESTION: **When we say this, do we mean that every
American official and every American source
of information thus follow the Communist
line?**

ANSWER: Certainly not. There are some officials and
some sources of information that were intelligent enough and alert enough to oppose
the line. But by and large, the line was far
too successful in bringing about the great
retreats and defeats for the United States
during the past twenty-five years.

21. QUESTION: **Can you give a striking example of the victory of the Communist line by consent of
the United States Government?**

ANSWER: Of the many that could be cited, the one
that first comes to mind is the recognition of
Soviet Russia by the United States in 1933.
This gave to atheistic Communism and its
representatives a prestige on which they
built their continued conquest of great sections of the globe.

22. QUESTION: **At this time, were we given examples of Soviet perfidy in connection with our Govern-
ment's agreeing to follow the Communist
line?**

ANSWER: We were indeed: a perfidy which has dis-
tinguished all Soviet acts. For one thing, in
the Roosevelt-Litvinov Pact of recognition,
Soviet Russia agreed solemnly and in writing to end all subversive activities in the
United States. This, of course, turned out to

be a farce, since the Communist Party of the United States appeared in 1935 at the Seventh World Congress of the Communist International and joined with the other parties in acclaiming Stalin as "the leader, teacher, and guide of the proletariat and oppressed of the whole world."

23. QUESTION: **Were there any other Communist acts at this time which showed the dishonest character of this agreement on the part of the Kremlin?**

ANSWER: Most decidedly. Several months before the Roosevelt-Litvinov agreement was signed, the Communist Party here had received instructions from Moscow to Sergei I. Gussev, who had operated here as Communist International representative under the name of P. Green. This directive from Moscow led to the famous "Open Letter to the Party," ordering infiltration into every area of American life. It was then that infiltration began on a large scale in the Government (this being the time when Alger Hiss and his co-conspirators of the Washington "cell" entered the Government).

24. QUESTION: **Was there any other feature of this Roosevelt-Litvinov agreement which showed that Soviet Russia could not be trusted at any time?**

ANSWER: There was indeed. For as was to be the case right along in Soviet-American relations, the Kremlin was to persuade us that everything it wanted us to do was in order to obtain "peace." That is what President Roosevelt and "President" Kalinin declared in exchanging notes agreeing to the act of recognition. At that very time, both **Inprecor (International Press Correspondence,** the Communist International reportorial agency at that time for the comrades) and the **Daily Worker** in this country declared that real peace could never come except by the overthrow of the capitalist system and those countries which supported it.

25. QUESTION: **How does the Communist line come to this country?**

ANSWER: a) By the Communist International representative, who functions in the shadow of the United States, directing the Communist Party here from Moscow. b) By means of the publications sent throughout the world from Moscow (and now Peking) and by their echoes in the United States, designed for American Communist consumption.

26. QUESTION: **Were the names of the Communist International Representatives known in the past to the Government of the United States?**

ANSWER: They have not only come to be known, but the list of them down to Gerhart Eisler and J. Peters, the latter of whom instructed Whittaker Chambers in espionage in Washington, have been published by the Senate Sub-Committee on Internal Security. These names can be obtained from the Research Department of that Senate Sub-Committee.

27. QUESTION: **Are the publications which convey the line from Moscow and Peking known, and can they be readily obtained?**

ANSWER: They are well known, and can be obtained in English editions in at least three main Communist book stores in mid-Manhattan, New York.

28. QUESTION: **What are these publications?**

ANSWER: At this period they are: **The World Marxist Review,** which goes into 83 countries in their respective tongues each month and is the chief directive-giver. **International Affairs** and **New Times,** going regularly to the 83 countries from Moscow itself. And then, in the United States, **Political Affairs,** the official theoretical organ of the Party and formerly known as the **The Communist,** and **The Worker,** which is the telegraph agency of the conspiracy to its active followers.

29. QUESTION: **How does the Communist line originate, in order that it be carried forward by these publications?**

ANSWER: It originates in the "report" of the dictator of Soviet Russia, who is also the leader of world Communism, to the various "congresses" of the Communist Party of the Soviet Union. Today the line throughout the world is based on the "report" of Dictator Nikita Khrushchev to the 20th and 21st Congresses of the Communist Party of the Soviet Union. The first of these was held in February, 1956, and the second in January, 1959.

30. QUESTION: **What are the main features of the current Communist line?**

ANSWER: a) "Face to face meetings between the leaders of the East and West," in order that thereby the United States will be pledged in

world opinion to acquiescence in the en-
slavement of the peoples behind the Iron
Curtain. This had been achieved in the visit
of Dictator Khrushchev to the United States,
by which in effect we put our sanction on
the slaughter of the Hungarians and the tyranny over the captive nations. At least that
was the impression made by the visit on people from behind the Iron Curtain.

b) "Cultural exchanges," a big feature of
the February, 1956 "report" by Dictator
Khrushchev. This is designed to expand the
Soviet espionage—military, political, and industrial—which formerly produced such
servants of the Kremlin as Alger Hiss in the
Government and the Rosenbergs. This process is now going forward, and the United
States is now wide open to Soviet espionage
against our country.

c) The final breaking down of all security
precautions in the United States against the
Communist conspiracy, by making permanent
the American superstition engendered by the
Reds in "the battle against McCarthyism."
This has now gone so far as the result of the
Supreme Court decisions, which have been
criticized by the American Bar Association,
that the United States is now without internal security protection of any real kind.

d) Persuading the United States to go to a
"Summit meeting," which has been a big
item in the current Communist line. It is designed to achieve at least two purposes: 1) to
attain new Communist conquest in Asia,

Africa, or Latin America while the United
States is distracted by long talks which
come to no agreement, and 2) to create serious rifts among the Western Powers, particularly possible since Great Britain seems constantly given to the appeasement tendency.

e) To get the United States eventually to
make such concessions on West Berlin and
West Germany as to make certain the final
achievement of a Soviet Germany and therefore of a Soviet Europe.

f) To persuade the United States to agree to
the recognition of Red China and to the ad-
mission of that barbarous regime into the
United Nations, in order to make easier the
Communist conquest of all Asia and also
Red dominance in Latin America, where the
"prestige" of Red China is being used in
Moscow's infiltration.

g) Strengthening of the Communist Party in
this country by complete failure to do anything substantial against that conspiracy and
by the encouragement to appeasement
raised by the Khrushchev visit. This is to be
accompanied by a great campaign for the
infiltration of the youth of the nation, first
by getting them to adopt features of the
Communist line and then by getting key
figures among the young people to become
secret Marxists.

31. QUESTION: **Is it possible to know and thereby combat
the Communist line?**

ANSWER: Most decidedly. That is our main current re-
sponsibility. It can be done by following the

pamphlets and articles that we and others write, by learning each week from the column by Louis F. Budenz, "The Reds, What Now?" appearing in many Catholic newspapers and by reading articles and books prepared by authorities who know from study and experience the policies and programs of Communism.

CHAPTER IV

THE COMMUNIST ATTITUDE
TOWARD REFORMS

1. QUESTION: **Do the Communists claim to be fervid champions of reforms?**

   ANSWER: Most decidedly. They claim constantly, in almost a chant, that they are in the "forefront" of the battle for the trade unions, in the struggle for the colonial peoples, and for Negro rights, and against anti-Semitism.

2. QUESTION: **Why, then, do the Communists constantly condemn the "reformists"?**

   ANSWER: Because the reformists actually believe in the reforms they advocate, whereas Communists advance reforms only in order to forward the Communist line and then to bring about the dictatorship.

3. QUESTION: **Has Pope Pius XI specifically called our attention to the hypocritical use by the Communists of reforms for their own subversive purposes?**

   ANSWER: Yes, His Holiness has done so in a number of places in his Encyclical on **Atheistic Communism,** warning us to cultivate "distrust of Communist tactics." In one sentence on this subject, he says: "Without receding an inch from their subversive principles, they invite Catholics to collaborate with them in the realm of so-called humanitarianism and charity; and at times even make proposals that are in perfect harmony with the Christian spirit and the doctrine of the Church."

4. QUESTION: **Are these warnings of the Pope justified by the experiences of the last forty years with the Soviet dictatorship?**

ANSWER: They are. Whenever Soviet Power establishes itself, it not only betrays its promises of reform but turns these promises into their opposites.

5. QUESTION: **Can you give outstanding examples of this experience?**

ANSWER: Yes, for there are many. Thus wherever the Soviet dictatorship sets itself up it abolishes free trade unions and does not permit collective bargaining or the right to strike. When it gets control of any colonial or colored people, as in China, its so-called "liberation" of them is actually the extention and intensification of slavery. From the time of Marx to Khrushchev, the Communist movement and Soviet Power have also carried forward and stimulated subtle and effective anti-Semitism.

6. QUESTION: **Has the trade union movement of this country recognized the hypocritical attitude of Soviet Communism toward the rights of the free trade unions?**

ANSWER: Yes. On many occasions. Specifically, in September, 1959, the Executive Council of the AFL-CIO refused to meet with Dictator Khrushchev when he was on his mission to spread appeasement in the United States.

The overwhelming vote in favor of this re-
jection of any contact with Khrushchev was
based on the fact that he represented a
regime which suppressed the free trade
unions.

7. QUESTION: **Can you cite one other striking illustration,
from out of experiences in this country with-
in trade unions, that justify this labor condemnation of the Soviet dictatorship?**

ANSWER: In 1950, this condemnation was brought out
strikingly by several committees of the Congress of Industrial Organizations (then a
separate body), when these committees presented reports on Red-ruled unions within
the CIO. Each committee recommended the
expulsion of these Red-ruled unions from the
Congress of Industrial Organizations.

8. QUESTION: **What was the indictment against the Communists in their operations in the trade
unions, which formed the heart of these
reports?**

ANSWER: In each report, it was stated: "The committee finds that the fundamental purpose of
the Communist Party is to promote the interests of the Soviet Union. It finds that,
although the Communist Party has claimed
to champion unionism and organization, it
has always done so in order to carry on
Communist work to pervert their policies to
the advantage of the Soviet Union. The
Communist Party, the committee finds, does
not believe in trade unions. It believes in
using trade unions. And it believes in using
them for the purposes of the Soviet Union."

9. QUESTION: **Is this Communist method of using reforms without actually believing in them a direct result of the Communist world view?**

   ANSWER: It is. For under that view—as Lenin states in **State and Revolution**—no genuine freedom is possible until the Communist society has been won. Since this Communist society cannot be gained without the achievement of the dictatorship, according to Marxism-Leninism, all mass organizations are expendable in the struggle to set up the dictatorship. The trade unions, for example, are of no consequence in themselves; they are for the Communists merely convenient agencies to achieve the aims of the vanguard.

10. QUESTION: **Has this concept of using reforms merely as a means to advance the Communist line and bring about the dictatorship been emphasized in any authoritative Red document?**

   ANSWER: Outstanding in this respect, there is the great Communist guide book of theory and tactics written by Joseph Stalin. This contains one whole sub-section dealing with "Reformism and Revolutionism," contained in the **Foundations of Leninism.**

11. QUESTION: **How does Stalin distinguish between the advocacy of reforms by a mere reformist and the same advocacy by a revolutionary or Communist?**

   ANSWER: He shows very clearly from the Communist viewpoint that "to a reformist, reforms are everything." But the Communist "will accept a reform in order to use it as an aid in combining legal work with illegal work, to intensify under its cover, the illegal work for the revolutionary preparation of the masses for the overthrow of the bourgeoisie."

12. QUESTION: **What does this mean to us?**

ANSWER: It means that the Communists will seek to enter every movement in non-Soviet countries which aims at establishing the rights of the trade unions or Negro rights or oppose anti-Semitism. It means it will use this penetration and participation to induce certain thoughtless people to throw the mantle of protection around the Communist conspiracy here. The excuse will be that the Communists will stand for "progress," a word which the Reds frequently use.

13. QUESTION: **Was this misuse of reforms to advance the Communist cause presented to the comrades in the United States by any guide for infiltration?**

ANSWER: It was. This method of using reforms as a means to advance the Communist cause was recommended as a model for working secretly in all organizations by John Williamson, a member of the American Politburo, in the November, 1950, issue of **Political Affairs.**

14. QUESTION: **What is the "American Politburo" and what is "Political Affairs"?**

ANSWER: The "Politburo" is the governing agency of the Communist Party in the United States, modeled after the Politburo in Moscow, which is now known as the Praesidium. It is now known as the National Executive Committee, as the Communists frequently change the names of their organizational units to confuse American investigations and discussions.

Political Affairs is the official theoretical organ of the Communist Party, formerly known as **The Communist.**

15. QUESTION: **What is the concealed individual Communist (or the concealed Red cell) in an organization told by Williamson to do first of all?**

ANSWER: The individual concealed Communist (or the members of the Red cell) must look around for "immediate needs" upon which he can base agitation. He must seek out those grievances or arguments which will appeal to those around him as non-Communist in character; that is the meaning of "immediate needs" or "immediate demands."

16. QUESTION: **What is he supposed to do after he has raised these "immediate needs" as a base for getting action?**

ANSWER: According to Williamson and the Communist tactics at all times, the concealed Communist is obliged to link up these "immediate needs" with the line of the Party, with those things which the Kremlin wants done in America at that particular period.

17. QUESTION: **Whom is the concealed Communist supposed to persuade to forward the line of the Party in an organization which is being penetrated?**

ANSWER: He is supposed to persuade willing non-Communists to bring forward the line of the

Party, so that it will not be recognized generally as the Communist and so that the Communist himself will not be "exposed" as a Communist.

18. QUESTION: **By methods of this sort, have the Communists been able to penetrate originally non-Communist organizations and get them to advance the Communist line?**

ANSWER: Yes. This has been done in many cases. An outstanding illustration is the successful penetration of the Institute of Pacific Relations, which was used as the fulcrum to influence our State Department to betray the Chinese people into Red Chinese hands.

19. QUESTION: **How was this done?**

ANSWER: It was done by the Communists taking control of the executive staff, which in an organization like the Institute of Pacific Relations is the decisive agency. The busy industrialists, lawyers, and university presidents on the boards and committees were manipulated by the executive and technical staffs, which were loaded down with Communists or those under Communist influences.

20. QUESTION: **How did this whole maneuver in the IPR fit in with the use of reforms to advance the Communist line?**

ANSWER: Those wealthy and influential non-Communists who joined the IPR did so under the belief that they were forwarding good will among the nations in the Pacific and also helping to ameliorate the harsh conditions of colonial rule. Instead, as extensive hearings by the Senate Sub-Committee on Internal Security in the early 1950's showed, they were being used to get our State Department and Government in general to assist in the fastening of Red Chinese tyranny on the mainland of China.

21. QUESTION: **Was enough public sentiment organized in America by the Communists, favorable to the false idea that the Reds stood for reforms in themselves, to bring about other victories for the Communist line?**

ANSWER: That by and large is the history of the last twenty-five years. As outstanding examples there was the American acquiescence in the betrayal of all the nations now behind the iron curtain into Soviet hands, at the end of World War II.

There was also the "compelling" of the United States to go to the summit conference in Geneva in 1955. While we talked there endlessly, Soviet Russia made its breakthrough into the Middle East.

In like manner was the United States also "forced" to go to Geneva in 1959 and to invite Dictator Nikita Khrushchev to our own country in the same year.

Every one of these steps, and many more, were hatched in Moscow, with instructions given to support them to the Communists of the eighty-three countries in which they operate. Then, in time, the United States bowed to Moscow's will in each case.

22. QUESTION: **Has a clear distinction been made between reforms, including the right to organize and**

the struggle against discrimination, and the Communist line?

ANSWER: There has, in the various Papal Encyclicals on the social question, including specifically **Quadragesimo Anno** and **Divini Redemptoris** by Pope Pius XI.

REFERENCES AND SUGGESTED READINGS:

Reports and Hearings of the Senate Sub-Committee on Internal Security and House Committee on Un-American Activities, which deal with Communist penetration and Communist fronts. The student will have to write for those documents now available to: Research Department, Senate Sub-Committee on Internal Security, Senate Office Building, Washington, D.C. Also, to Francis E. Walter, Chairman, House Committee on Un-American Activities, House Office Building, Washington, D.C.

Above all: Consult Report by Senate Sub-Committee on Internal Security on the Institute of Pacific Relations, July 2, 1952.

The student can also write President George Meany, AFL-CIO, AFL Building, Washington, D.C., for copies of official labor reports dealing with the Communist menace to the unions.

CHAPTER V

THE CATHOLIC CHURCH
AND COMMUNISM

1. QUESTION: Has the Catholic Church explained and refuted the serious errors of Marxism?

ANSWER: Yes! Early and frequently. In 1846 Pius IX pronounced a solemn condemnation of "that infamous doctrine of so-called Communism, which is absolutely contrary to the natural law, and if once adopted would utterly destroy the rights, property and possessions of all men, and even Society itself." (This was two years before the **Communist Manifesto** was published.)

In 1878 Pope Leo XIII defined Communism as: "The fatal plague which insinuates itself into the marrow of human society, only to bring about its ruin."

The Supreme Pontiff Pius XI, prior to 1937, wrote nine official documents on the evils of Communism. On March 19th, 1937, his renowned Encyclical on "Atheistic Communism" was widely acclaimed in all free nations. It is an excellent summary of Marxism-Leninism.

2. QUESTION: **What did Pius XI say of this "Bolshevistic and Atheistic Communism?"**

ANSWER: That "the all too imminent danger" of our own days is "Bolshevistic and Atheistic

Communism, which aims at upsetting the social order and at undermining the very foundations of Christian civilization."

3. QUESTION: **How did Pius XI characterize this "Atheistic Communism?"**

ANSWER: As a "satanic scourge," carrying on throughout the world "diabolical propaganda."

4. QUESTION: **Upon what did Pius XI further say Communism builds its strength?**

ANSWER: It "conceals in itself a false messianic idea" shot through "with a deceptive mysticism, which communicates a zealous and contagious enthusiasm to the multitudes entrapped by delusive promises."

(Of course, both this "false messianic idea" and "deceptive mysticism" arise from the two-fold false promises of Marxism-Leninism: A. That injustice to the workers shall be remedied when the "dictatorship of the proletariat" or socialism is established, and B. That when this dictatorship "withers away," it will be succeeded by the earthly paradise of the Communist society.)

5. QUESTION: **Was the way prepared for Communism by preceding anti-religious doctrines?**

ANSWER: Yes; Pius XI points out that in days past groups of "intellectuals" were formed "in an arrogant attempt to free civilization from the bonds of morality and religion." Always the preceding Popes had drawn the attention of the world to the subsequent "consequences of the de-Christianization of human society."

(These "philosophies" were also accompanied by such movements as Grand Orient Free Masonry and the Illuminati.)

6. QUESTION: **What further description of Communism is found in the 1937 Encyclical?**

   ANSWER: Its propaganda "so truly diabolical that the world perhaps never witnessed its like before" is directed "from one common center." Then we read: "It is shrewdly adapted to the varying conditions of diverse peoples. It has at its disposal great financial resources, gigantic organizations, international congresses, and countless trained workers. It makes use of pamphlets and reviews, of cinema, theatre and radio, of schools and even universities."

7. QUESTION: **How then does the Pope tell us it carries on its penetrations, forwarding what we have learned is "the Communist line?"**

   ANSWER: Here is the literal statement of Pius XI: "Little by little it penetrates into all classes of the people and even reaches the better-minded groups of the community, with the result that few are aware of the poison which increasingly pervades their minds and hearts."

8. QUESTION: **Does this mean, as the Pope puts it, that even believers in God, including Catholics, can sometimes be tricked into following the Communist line?**

   ANSWER: Most decidedly, and that is why Pius XI devoted a whole section of his encyclical to warning against the "trickery in various forms" used by the Communists. It was because of this that His Holiness warned, speaking to the Bishops: "See to it, Venerable Brethren, that the faithful do not allow themselves to be deceived! Communism is intrinsically wrong, and no one who would save Christian civilization may collaborate with it in any undertaking whatsoever."

9. QUESTION: **Why did Pius XI brand Communism as "intrinsically wrong" and a "satanic scourge?"**

   ANSWER: Because Communism as a philosophy of life is evil in its very nature: always, everywhere, and in all its essential features.

10. QUESTION: **Why is Communism intrinsically evil?**

   ANSWER: Because it is materialistic and atheistic. It is a denial of human spiritual dignity, human rights, and human freedom.

11. QUESTION: **Have "the great Communist scientists," Marx, Engels, Lenin and Stalin, acknowledged this fundamental materialistic (and therefore atheistic) character of Communism?**

   ANSWER: Each one of them in turn has proclaimed materialism as the foundation stone of all the other Communist tenets. Thus, Frederick Engels in his work, **Ludwig Feuerbach,** makes the assault on all belief in God the very heart of that work. Thus V. I. Lenin in his booklet, **The Teachings of Karl Marx,** which is widely distributed by the Communists in America today, makes materialism and the materialistic conception of the world the basis for all of the Marxist ideas. And thus Joseph V. Stalin, in chapter 4 of his **History of the Communist Party of the Soviet Union,** states emphatically in a phrase often quoted by the Communists: "Dialectical materialism is the world outlook of the Marxist-Leninist Party."

12. QUESTION: **What attitude does this materialism lead the Communists to take in regard to religion?**

ANSWER: One of the utmost hostility, which leads to the determination to destroy religion, sometimes by weakening it through divisions and sometimes by stamping it out by force.

As Lenin says in vol. 11 of his **Selected Works** (page 664): "Religion is the opium of the people—this dictum of Marx's is the cornerstone of the whole Marxist view on religion. Marxism has always regarded all modern religions and churches and all religious organizations as instruments of bourgeois reaction that serve to defend exploitation and to drug the working class."

13. QUESTION: **Apart from Russia, have we any proof that Communism is a brutal system of inhuman cruelty, tyranny and religious hatred?**

ANSWER: Yes, we have many such proofs. That is the story in every country behind the iron curtain. It has been signalized in Soviet perfidy and brutality exhibited in the massacre of the Hungarian freedom fighters. It has been seen in the killing off of thousands in China, as lately as 1958, in the "rectification campaign." Against the Catholic Church, this has been evidenced in the enforced schism in China and in the taking over by Soviet Power of the apparatus of the Church in Hungary.

14. QUESTION: **Did Pius XI bring forward such proofs in his Encyclical?**

ANSWER: Yes. a) The horrible persecutions of Christians in Mexico in 1910 and after, where Catholic Churches were destroyed, priests arrested and put to death; the Catholic press was suppressed and violence tolerated. b) The Spanish Civil War in the early thirties: In this Soviet-sponsored revolution, planned for more than thirty years, with diabolic propaganda preceding, anti-clericism was featured and numerous conflicting political parties were organized by the International Conspirators. Several hundred Catholic Churches were destroyed; and thousands of Catholic priests, nuns, and social workers were killed. (Millions of non-combatants perished, but Spain was saved by the grace of God, by deep faith and heroic courage, under the leadership of Franco.)

15. QUESTION: **How did Pius XI explain the origin, success and popular appeal of a system which is intrinsically wrong?**

ANSWER: The saintly Pontiff advanced several basic reasons which are as valid today as they were 32 years ago. Namely: a) Every error seems to contain an element of truth; e.g., the Bolshevists stress the evils of private enterprise. b) Most persons are not aware of the insidious evils of Marxism. c) The young, especially, are not well informed about the

satanic nature of Communism. d) The false
intellectuals and liberals regarded Marxism
as a new Socio-Economic System worthy of
their support.

16. QUESTION: **What is the meaning, incidentally, of "Bol-
shevist" or "Bolshevik?"**

ANSWER: It means "a member of the majority," not al-
luding to the majority among the people.
The Communists or Marxist-Leninist Party,
as Lenin organized it on the basis of the
Marxian ideas, must always be a small group
imposing their will by guile and infiltration
in the first place and then by force upon the
people of any country. The word "majority,"
as used here, refers to the fact that the followers of V. I. Lenin received a majority
vote on certain points in an important socialist convention in London, held some years
before the Revolution in Russia.

17. QUESTION: **What part did Pius XI say "a large section of
the non-Catholic press" played in the spread
and success of Marxism-Leninism?**

ANSWER: On this important issue, the same illustrious
Pontiff said: "A third powerful factor in the
diffusion of Communism is the conspiracy of
silence on the part of a large section of the
non-Catholic press of the world." At that
time, he pointed out that this "conspiracy"
had been evidenced by: a) The failure of
many papers to expose the horror perpetrat-
ed in Russia, in Mexico, and even in a great
part of Spain; b) the failure of many to in-
dict as they could "a world organization as

vast as Russian Communism," upon whose repugnant aspects so many journals remained silent.

18. QUESTION: **Is this indictment by Pius XI of "a large section of the non-Catholic press" still applicable to many of our general or secular journals?**

ANSWER: Unfortunately, it is, even to the point where we seldom see any intelligent and popular indictment of the "Marxist-Leninist classics," which would enlighten the American people at once on the fact that the very nature of Communism makes it impossible for us to deal with it except for our ruination.

In addition, in many of our leading secular journals, we see no references to the publications from Moscow and Peking, sent to the Communists here steadily, and an examination of which would alert the American people in advance to the Communist line.

19. QUESTION: **Did the Government of the United States help the cause of Communism in Spain and elsewhere at this time (1932-1937)?**

ANSWER: Decidedly. It allowed the "Abraham Lincoln Brigade" openly and illegally to recruit American soldiers for service in the Loyalist (i.e. Marxist) army. It encouraged reds, pinkos and fellow-travellers to circulate widely their misleading propaganda and to attack publicly General Franco and the defenders of religious and civic freedom in Spain.

20. QUESTION: **Did the Government of the United States also help to build up Soviet Communist rule**

over other places by its policies of appeasement?

ANSWER: Yes. As has been previously indicated, from
1933 on, the Government of the United
States, with the exception of the few years of
the Hitler-Stalin Pact (1939-1941) has acquiesced in the brutal establishment of Soviet
rule over every country now behind the Iron
Curtain.

21. QUESTION: **What did Pius XI recommend to the Catholic press by way of advancing social study
and offsetting Communism?**

ANSWER: He strongly advised the Catholic press to
play a prominent part in the following
moves: a) "to foster in various attractive
ways an ever better understanding of social
doctrine," which of course meant engaging
in the championship of social reform of
a sound character for the working classes;
b) to supply "accurate and complete information on the activity of the (Communist)
enemy and the means of resistance found
most effective in various quarters;" and c)
to "warn against the insidious deceits with
which Communists endeavor all too success-
fully to attract even men of good faith."
(It can be seen that Pius XI is urging here a
particular crusade of enlightenment in the
Catholic press on the Communist line.)

22. QUESTION: **Did Pius XI counsel positive action for Christian charity and social justice in addition to
recommending intelligent and vigilant action against Communism as it actually oper-
ates?**

ANSWER: Most emphatically. In turn and at some length, he emphasized: a) The renewal of Christian life as the basis for all social reform and as answering the atheism of Communism; b) the pursuit of Christian charity, which would not only include helping those who are in difficulties but also in leading "a more moderate way of life;" c) the strict following out of Christian social justice, as stressed so definitely in Pius XI's Encyclical **Quadragesimo Anno,** to which he referred again, and also in Leo XIII's **Rerum Novarum** (On the Condition of Labor).

23. QUESTION: **In connection with this emphasis on social justice, did Pius XI mention specifically the rights of the labor movement and the deplorable acts of "those Catholic industrialists" who try to block the right to organize?**

ANSWER: Yes, he singled out for criticism "certain Catholic circles" who have "refused to understand that Christian charity demands the recognition of certain rights due to the working man, which the Church has explicitly acknowledged." And His Holiness continued: "Is it not deplorable that the right of private property defended by the Church should so often have been used as a weapon to defraud the working man of his just salary and his social rights?"

24. QUESTION: **How did Catholics, generally, react to the Papal teaching on Communism?**

ANSWER: The majority of Catholics throughout the world accepted these truths on Atheistic

Communism (Marxism-Leninism), gratefully and with great concern. But millions of devout Catholics soon forgot the essentials of the Encyclical and failed to seek further knowledge about it. Many did not study the Encyclical, and the other pronouncements of the Papacy on social questions, in order to put them into action. In a word, they did not examine them and learn from them to the same extent that the Communists learned from the "Marxist-Leninist classics"—the teachings of Marx, Engels, Lenin, Stalin, Mao Tse-tung, and now Khrushchev.

25. QUESTION: **Did Pius XI recommend the study of social problems as enunciated by the Papal Encyclicals?**

ANSWER: That is one of the chief features of Pius XI's counsels: The promotion of "a wider study of social problems in the light of the doctrine of the Church." This social study and propaganda were urged for two chief reasons: a) To disseminate widely the social teachings of the Church in a positive sense (such as the right to organize, championship of the just rights of the Negro people, Christian opposition to anti-Semitism, legislation favorable to the just claims of the working classes), and b) to understand the nature, the tactics, and the trickery of the Communist enemy.

26. QUESTION: **What is one of the great dangers for the Catholics in America that we can learn from these counsels and repeated warnings of Pius XI?**

ANSWER: Not so much that they will embrace Communism in itself, at least immediately, as they have some sense of its atheistic and inherently tyrannical character, but that they will, in large numbers, fall victim to the Communist line, being deceived into doing what Moscow wants them to do because it is presented under non-Communist and sometimes "American" colors.

(That is why it is the part of wisdom to read again Chapter III on the Communist line, to be sure it is thoroughly grasped.)

REFERENCES AND SUGGESTED READINGS:

Belloc, Hilaire. **The Servile State.** London: Constable and Co.
The Restoration of Property. New York: Sheed and Ward.

Fanfani, Amintore. **Catholicism, Protestantism, and Capitalism.** London: Sheed and Ward.

Great Encyclical Letters of Leo XIII. New York: Benziger Brothers.

Husslein, Joseph, S.J. **Social Wellsprings.** Milwaukee: Bruce Pub. Co.
volume 1 **Encyclicals and Social Reconstruction,** Leo XIII
volume 2 **Social Encyclicals of Pius XI.**

CHAPTER VI

COMMUNISM AND RELIGION

1. QUESTION: **Can Communism rightly be called a religion?**

   ANSWER: No. Religion means the worship of God, by man. Communism is a complete denial of our dependence on the Supreme Being. As an illustration, Frederick Engels in summing up the teaching of dialectical materialism in his book, **Ludwig Feuerbach,** shows that Marxism does not permit the slightest concession to religion or to any entering wedge for belief in the Divinity. Engels actually criticizes the materialist Feuerbach for not being materialistic enough.

2. QUESTION: **How does Karl Marx himself express the Communist view of religion?**

   ANSWER: He writes in words which have been quoted throughout the world: "Religion is the sigh of the oppressed creature, the sentiment of a heartless world, as it is the spirit of spiritless condition. It is the opium of the people ... The criticism of religion is the beginning of all criticism."

3. QUESTION: **Is this hostile view of religion continued and confirmed by V. I. Lenin?**

   ANSWER: Yes. This concept of religion runs throughout the whole of Volume XI of Lenin's **Se-**

lected Works. As an instance, we read on page 663: "The philosophical basis of Marxism, as Marx and Engels repeatedly declared, is dialectical materialism, which fully embodies the historical traditions of the materialism of the eighteenth century in France and of Feuerbach (first half of the nineteenth century) in Germany—a materialism which is absolutely atheistic and resolutely hostile to all religion."

4. QUESTION: **Has Lenin expressed this hostility to religion in other forms?**

ANSWER: He has, indeed. He has declared that the Communist Party is the Party of "militant atheism" and that any Marxist journal must be a journal of "militant atheism." Further than that, in his **Letters to A. M. Gorky,** Lenin has written (page 675 of Volume XI of his **Selected Works**): "Every religious idea, every idea of god, even every flirtation with the idea of god, is unutterable vileness."

5. QUESTION: **Why is Marxism-Leninism called "militant atheism?"**

ANSWER: Because it engages in every conceivable form of hostility to crush religion: a) enlisting the enthusiasm and zeal of Communists in hatred of religion to the point where it becomes fanaticism; b) organizing false propaganda and brute force in the persecution of religious persons and the suppression of religious organizations by military oppression; and c) employing deceit in its most extreme form to create schisms in religious groups and to set one division of a religious organization against another, thus encouraging disintegration and disbelief.

6. QUESTION: **Why do Marxists oppose religion?**

   ANSWER: Marx, Engels, Lenin, Stalin, and all present-day Communists charge that religion dulls the mind in regard to economic ills, poverty, and suffering; that the promise of happiness in heaven is a conscious deception of the masses by Bishops, priests, and ministers of religion.

   Today, the Marxists accuse the Churches of condoning the evils of capitalism and of being apologists for "the imperialists" and "the bourgeoisie." These charges are offset simply by an examination of the Papal Encyclicals.

7. QUESTION: **How do Communists explain the existence of beliefs and experiences that are spiritual in character?**

   ANSWER: They say quite cynically that these manifestations are merely the super-structure of existing things, which arise from the sub-structure of "reality" which is completely materialistic. For instance, in history, they claim that each ruling class in each period brings forth its own form of religion and law to aid in the oppression of the lower classes.

8. QUESTION: **Is there any refutation in history to such a contention?**

   ANSWER: Yes, there are many. We will take one, the Catholic Church itself. It has existed and functioned under the slave state, feudalism, and capitalism in succession.

9. QUESTION: **Why, then, cannot religion, and specifically the Catholic Church, have a free existence under Communism?**

ANSWER: Because Communism, either in its first stage of socialism which it claims has been reached today in the "socialist countries," or in its alleged and hypothetical "higher state" of the Communist society, must of its very nature carry on subtle and open persecutions of the Church. In this way, it truly fulfills its role of a "satanic scourge."

10. QUESTION: **What is the status of the Catholic Church in Russia under Communism?**

ANSWER: The Catholic religion in Russia since the 1917 Revolution has been practically suppressed. A few Catholic Churches remain open for worship in the larger cities, but there are no priests to administer the Sacraments or to offer Mass. Most Catholic Churches in Russia have been destroyed, closed, or taken over by the Soviets.

11. QUESTION: **Has the Russian Orthodox Church fared better than the Catholic Church?**

ANSWER: Yes, in some ways. Its members are more numerous, and influential. Hence, the Soviets did not try to eradicate the Orthodox religion, but to control it. The Patriarch and Orthodox Bishops cannot function without Soviet approval, or oppose in any way the feared and detested Communist regime.
Note: The number of Protestants in Russia is comparatively small.

12. QUESTION: **Has religion been treated in the same way in other countries under Soviet tyranny?**

ANSWER: Wherever the Communists are in power, the attacks on religion, particularly against Catholics, continue effectively. For example, in Poland, Eastern Germany, Rumania, Lithuania, and Hungary the intent is the same as in Russia, but the strategy and methods of opposition vary for political reasons.

In the Ukraine, Catholic priests today are being arrested and sent into Siberia; in China, Bishops are being compelled to consecrate other "bishops" in defiance of the Vatican, thereby creating a schism. In Hungary, where Cardinal Mindszenty has been so severely persecuted, the Communist Party is asserting the "right" to appoint Bishops and even parish priests.

13. QUESTION: **In recent years, and at present, has the hostility to religion lessened or increased?**

ANSWER: There has been no important change. The 1936 Soviet Constitution is still the law of the land, and was reprinted in English in 1956 by the Foreign Languages Publishing House of Moscow; also in many other languages.

14. QUESTION: **What does this alleged Constitution say about religion?**

ANSWER: Article 124 reads: "In order to ensure to citizens freedom of conscience, the church in the U.S.S.R. is separated from the state, and the school from the church. Freedom of religious worship and freedom of anti-religious propaganda is recognized for all citizens."

15. QUESTION: **What does this Article 124 mean in reality?**

ANSWER: It means, as we have stated, that religion is suppressed in Soviet Russia, except where it serves the purposes of the Dictatorship to maintain a "front" of alleged religious freedom. This, we have seen, it does through the controlled Orthodox Church. The power to harass and handicap religion is entirely in the hands of the Soviet leaders, who are committed to the extension of atheism.

16. QUESTION: **Are certain features of this Article 124, therefore, hypocritical?**

ANSWER: Yes, as is the case with all the Articles dealing with alleged "rights" of Soviet citizens. These "rights" include, ironically enough, "freedom of speech, freedom of the press, freedom of assembly, including the holding of mass meetings, freedom of street processions and demonstrations."

And yet, according to the admissions of Nikita S. Khrushchev, made for his own purposes, at the 20th Congress of the Communist Party of the Soviet Union, 1956, these "rights" were so utterly disregarded as actually to be accompanied by one of the most revolting reigns of terror in history.

17. QUESTION: **Is Communism then, seeking to establish its "militant atheism" as a substitute for religion?**

ANSWER: That is precisely what it is doing by its "promise" to bring about the earthly paradise of the Communist society. To advance this aim, it calls upon the Communists to dedicate themselves to the utmost degree.

To this end, for instance, the Communist Parties of the world are distributing in every language a booklet entitled, **How To Be a Good Communist,** authored by Liu-Shao-chi, the present head of Red China. The theme of that booklet is that there must be "unconditional subordination of the personal interests of a Party member to the interests of the Party." Communists must even go to death with a smile on their faces for the sake of the Party.

REFERENCES:

The two chapters in Father McFadden's **Philosophy of Communism** dealing with Communism and religion.

Galter, Albert, **The Red Book of the Persecuted Church,** Newman Press, 1957.

Khrushchev, Nikita S., **The Crimes of the Stalin Era,** special report to the 20th Congress of the Communist Party of the Soviet Union, annotated by Boris I. Nicolaevsky, New Leader, New York, 1956.

CHAPTER VII

COMMUNISM AND MORALITY

1. QUESTION: **What is the Communist idea of morality?**

   ANSWER: It is expressed by the synthetic term, "class morality." That is, it is the worst form of the conception that the end justifies the means. Those words and actions which promote the achievement of the world Soviet dictatorship (and thereafter of the Communist society) are morally good. Whatever hinders this Soviet dictatorship (and the alleged consequent Communist society) is morally bad.

2. QUESTION: **Does this mean that murder, lying, and injustice are permitted by the Communists as something good?**

   ANSWER: Yes. If by these acts the cause of Communism will actually be advanced, these deeds are moral. If such acts do not advance Communism, they are immoral.

3. QUESTION: **Did any leading Communist "scientist" propound this view, early in the history of the Communist movement?**

   ANSWER: Yes. This was clearly defined by Frederick Engels in his celebrated work, **Anti-Duehring.**

4. QUESTION: **What did Engels say there?**

    ANSWER: Partly he declared: "We therefore reject every attempt to impose on us any moral dogma whatsoever as an external, ultimate and forever immutable moral law on the pretext that the moral world too has its permanent principles which transcend history and the differences between nations. We maintain on the contrary that all former moral theories are the product, in the last analysis, of the economic stage which society had reached at that particular epoch. And as society has hitherto moved in class antagonism, morality was always a class morality; it has either justified the domination and the interests of the ruling class, or, as soon as the oppressed class has become powerful enough, it has represented the revolt against this domination and the future interests of the oppressed."

    He therefore maintains that the only "morality" that existed was "class morality."

5. QUESTION: **Was this view by Engels later on underlined by any other Communist statement?**

    ANSWER: By many, but specifically by V. I. Lenin, his comments being published far and wide by the Communists in his pamphlet on **The Young Generation.** This is issued by the Little Lenin Library.

6. QUESTION: **What did Lenin state in that booklet?**

    ANSWER: There he declared: "We repudiate all morality derived from non-human and non-class concepts. We say that it is a deception, a fraud, a befogging of the minds of the work-

ers and peasants in the interests of the land-
lords and capitalists.

"We say that our morality is entirely sub-
ordinated to the interests of the class struggle of the proletariat. Our morality is derived from the interests of the class struggle
of the proletariat."

7. QUESTION: **Did Lenin define this "Communist morality"
still further?**

ANSWER: Yes. In the same pamphlet he goes on to say:
"When people talk to us about morality, we
say: for the Communist, morality lies entirely in this compact, united, disciplined and
conscious mass struggle against the exploit-
ers. We do not believe in an eternal morality, and we expose all the lying fables about
morality."

8. QUESTION: **Does this "morality" receive further defini-
tion in Lenin's instructions on infiltration?**

ANSWER: It does indeed. In giving instructions to the
Communists of the world on the infiltration
of the trade unions, which is always used by
the Marxists as the basis for the infiltration of all organizations, Lenin wrote:
"We must be able to withstand all this, to
agree to any sacrifice, and even—if need be—
to resort to all sorts of strategems, artifices,
illegal methods, to evasions and subterfuges,
only so as to get into the trade unions, to remain in them, and to carry on Communist
work within them at all costs."
This appears on p. 38 of **Left Wing Communism: An Infantile Disorder,** authored by
V. I. Lenin and issued by the Little Lenin
Library.

9. QUESTION: **Has this view of "morality" characterized the history of Communism up to date?**

ANSWER: It has. It marked the careers of Marx and Engels. But passing that over, as also the many examples we could quote from the life of Lenin, we will note that Stalin deliberately murdered several million Kulaks (middle-class Russian farmers) because they did not cooperate with the Collective (socialist) plans and program.

10. QUESTION: **Was this "morality" expressed by many other such acts of violence under Stalin's regime?**

ANSWER: It went to such an extent that Dictator Nikita S. Khrushshev, the new Stalin, for his own purposes had to expose some of the criminal acts which marked Stalin's rule. We must note that Khrushchev confined himself largely to the recitation of Stalin's murders and perfidy against "loyal Communists" and said practically nothing about Stalin's larger crimes against the Russian people.

This whole address of Khrushchev, given at the 20th Congress of the Communist Party of the Soviet Union, was reprinted in English. The editor of that edition, Anatole Shub, in his critical observations, said:

"Most significant, however, is the paradoxical dualism that runs through Khrushchev's address from start to finish: While Stalin's crimes against his Communist associates are vividly spelled out and deplored, his infinitely greater crimes against the Russian people are applauded in the name of 'socialist construction.' Khrushchev's 'anti-Stalin'

speech (like the official pronunciamentos
which followed) reaffirms the basic Stalinist
policy line explicitly and implicitly, although now it is affirmed in Lenin's name."

11. QUESTION: **While these and many other crimes were being committed by Stalin, what was the pic-
ture presented to the American nation?**

ANSWER: Through the Communist influences in our
press and radio, the American nation was
induced to believe that the "Stalin Constitution of 1936" was bringing about the "freedom" in Soviet Russia which it promised. We
were also induced to believe in World War
II that Soviet Russia was one of the "peaceful and democratic nations."

In twenty-five years, the American Government and American people have been lied to
by the Communists and their infiltrators to
the extent that we have acquiesced in the
gift of one-third of the world to Soviet
Power.

12. QUESTION: **Should Communists generally, and the Soviet rulers in particular, be trusted in regard
to the promises they make?**

ANSWER: No. First, because they will not make any
agreement or concession unless it helps
Communism. Secondly, after the promise or
concession is made, the Soviets will disregard
it if it does not work out in their favor.

13. QUESTION: **Does this mean that conferences at the
"Summit," or at a lower level such as at
Geneva, are a waste of time and money?**

ANSWER: They are worse than that, as the record of
such meetings clearly proves: for instance,

Yalta, Teheran, and Potsdam with their betrayal of several nations. Since 1917 the Soviets have made fifty-two official agreements with the Western Nations. Fifty of these have been flagrantly violated.

14. QUESTION: **Are so-called "Cultural Exchanges" between the Soviets and the United States of any practical value?**

ANSWER: They are to the Soviet leaders and to the cause of Marxism as the men of the Kremlin intend. They do not benefit the American people or government except in trivial ways. There are those who contend that some of the members of the Russian cultural groups are Soviet intelligence agents.

15. QUESTION: **In addition to the Soviet espionage—political, industrial, and military—furthered by "cultural exchanges," is there any other damage done by these exchanges?**

ANSWER: Most decidedly. These cultural exchanges were initiated as the policy (and part of the Communist line) by Nikita Khrushchev at the 20th Congress of the Communist Party of the Soviet Union precisely in order to injure America. These "exchanges" add to the number of appeasers in America, to the number of those who will forward the Communist line, and to the creation of that "atmosphere" of unguardedness which the Communist conspiracy is always forwarding in non-Soviet nations in order to weaken them.

16. QUESTION: **Does the Marxist theory of morality admit the existence of natural rights, such as the**

right to life, liberty and the pursuit of happiness?

ANSWER: According to the Marxist ideology, (i.e., their system and philosophy) there are actually no natural rights. Since the Communist Party is inevitably destined to establish world-wide Soviet dictatorship (socialism) and thence bring about entering into the Communist society, it is the Party which is the sole custodian and judge of the "rights" that can be granted to men. In practice, therefore, it is the socialist state, controlled by the Party, which is the source of any limited rights granted to its citizens.

17. QUESTION: That means, then, that the Soviet dictatorship, controlled by the Party and its leaders, can take any action to restrict the rights or liberties of the people?

ANSWER: That is correct. The State, controlled by the dictatorship of the Party, acting in the name of "the dictatorship of the proletariat," may and does restrict, deny, or destroy the right to own property, to hold free elections, and to religious worship, according to those decisions which are considered helpful to the Communist cause.

In contrast, "the bourgeois State," such as the United States of America, is to be hampered at every step. It is to be persuaded to take such an extreme and unrealistic attitude toward civil liberty as will allow the Communists to function freely in their subversive activities. It is regrettable that under the cry of "the battle against McCarthyism," the Communists have now made the United

States impotent so far as internal security is concerned.

18. QUESTION: Is it this peculiar view of the Communist Party as the custodian of "Communist morality" which makes veteran Communists confess to crimes they did not commit, when the Kremlin so orders?

ANSWER: That is the reason exactly. It has been brought out very interestingly by Arthur Koestler, a former Communist fellow traveler, in his novel, **Darkness at Noon.**

REFERENCES

The Crimes of the Stalin Era, by Nikita S. Khrushchev, Annotated by Boris I. Nicolaevsky, New Leader, New York.
The Mind of an Assassin, Isaac Don Levine, Farrar, Straus and Cudahy, New York, 1959.
Darkness at Noon, Arthur Koestler, Modern Library.
In the Name of Conscience, Nikolai Khokhlov, David McKay, New York, 1959.

CHAPTER VIII

COMMUNISM AND THE STATE

1. QUESTION: **What does Communism teach in regard to the State?**

   ANSWER: It teaches that the State in each period of history is the organ of power and suppression which the ruling, exploiting class calls into being in order to control the exploited and oppressed class. It is therefore always in Lenin's words "an organ of class domination, an organ of oppression of one class by another." It is always the dictatorship of the ruling class over the ruled.

2. QUESTION: **What is then the purpose and function of the State as the Communists see it?**

   ANSWER: The purpose of the State is primarily "the protection of private ownership," and the function of the State is the forcible maintaining of the exploited class in our day, the so-called proletariat in the position of economic slavery.

3. QUESTION: **Is the United States, as a current form of the present State, considered by the Communists to be a dictatorship?**

   ANSWER: Yes. It is one of the expressions of the "dictatorship of the bourgeoisie." Unions may be free to organize, as they are not permitted to do in Soviet Russia, workers may be permitted to strike, as they are forbidden to do under Soviet rule everywhere. But nevertheless, this must be in the Marxist theory and practice assessed as a dictatorship of the present ruling class, the so-called bourgeoisie.

4. QUESTION: **Does not this Communist view fly in the face of the facts?**

    ANSWER: Yes, it emphatically does. Like all Marxist assertions, it is based on an oversimplification of facts on the one hand and a crude distortion of them on the other to make those facts fit Marxist-Leninist theory.

5. QUESTION: **Are Soviet Russia and the so-called socialist countries also dictatorships?**

    ANSWER: Yes. The Communists openly acknowledge that they are dictatorships, but by the language of confusion to which the Communists constantly resort, they are called "democratic" dictatorships. In the alleged operation of the dialectical process in our present-day "capitalist society," the synthesis which must be worked out by the opposition of bourgeoisie and proletariat is the dictatorship of the proletariat. That is what the Communists say exists in Soviet Russia and the other so-called socialist countries.

6. QUESTION: **Is not this "dictatorship of the proletariat" actually the dictatorship of the Communist Party and its leaders?**

    ANSWER: Precisely. That is what both Lenin acknowledges, and Stalin re-emphasizes in his work **The Problems of Leninism.** To try to get

around this difficulty of calling the dictatorship of the Party the dictatorship of the proletariat, Stalin resorts to a play on words.

He asserts that the dictatorship of the proletariat is the dictatorship of the Communist
Party in **essence,** but **not wholly.**

7. QUESTION: **What does Stalin mean by this strange for-
mulation?**

ANSWER: With tongue in cheek, he explains solemnly
that the dictatorship of the proletariat is the
dictatorship of the Party **in essence** because
in that period the Party gives all the orders.
The proletariat, whose alleged dictatorship
it is, follows out these orders and carries
them among the general population.

Then, Stalin proceeds to say that the dictatorship of the proletariat is **not wholly** the
dictatorship of the Party precisely because
of this process. In other words, as so often in
Marxist-Leninist lore, Stalin is clearly attempting to cover up the stark fact that the
so-called dictatorship of the proletariat is in
reality only the dictatorship of the Communist Party and of its leaders.

8. QUESTION: **What are the two chief Communist books
which deal with the origin and nature of the
State?**

ANSWER: Although Marxist-Leninist literature con-
siders the nature and functions of the State
in many books and documents, the two chief
works on this subject are **The Origin of the
Family, Private Property and the State,** by
Frederick Engels; and **State and Revolution,**
by V. I. Lenin.

9. QUESTION: **What does Marxism-Leninism, speaking through Engels, assert concerning the origin of the State?**

ANSWER: It denies that the State arises from man's rational nature in requiring civil society and authority if large groups of human beings are to live together. This explanation of St. Thomas Aquinas is ignored by the Communists. On the other hand, Engels declares without proof that "all civilized peoples begin with the common ownership of the land." Then, in time, private property begins to appear and with it a class which possesses the property and a class which has little or none. In order to keep down this latter class, maintaining constantly its subservience and subjection, the exploiting class brings the State into being.

When in the course of history the exploited class overthrows the previous exploiting class, then it creates a new State in order to keep the additional class below it in servitude.

In addition, Marxism-Leninism contends that the Soviet socialist state will not be overthrown, as the expressions of the other "dictatorships" before it. On the contrary, the Soviet socialist state will voluntarily "wither away" into the Communist society. This will occur because under so-called socialism (now supposedly existing in Soviet Russia) there are no more exploited classes and consequently when this socialism becomes world-wide, there will be no need for a State.

10. QUESTION: But is not this assertion that "exploitation of man by man is ended" in Soviet Russia a lot of nonsense?

ANSWER: It is, indeed. This has been shown by many writers, including David Dallin in his book, **The Real Soviet Russia**, and Milovan Djilas' **The New Class.**

11. QUESTION: And yet, what does Marxism-Leninism—speaking through V. I. Lenin in his State and Revolution—predict will be the fate of the bourgeois and proletarian states respectively?

ANSWER: Lenin devotes his whole book (and it is an outstanding Marxist-Leninist "classic") to the alleged exposition of the fact that the capitalist or bourgeois State (including the Government of the United States specifically) must be overthrown by violence. The Soviet Socialist State, on the contrary, cannot be overthrown by violence. It must by evolution "wither away" into the Communist society.

12. QUESTION: What is the instrument to bring about the dictatorship of the proletariat, according to the Communists, and what agency will guide mankind to the Communist or classless society?

ANSWER: In his **Foundations of Leninism,** Stalin puts this matter succinctly. We quote: "The proletariat needs the (Communist) Party for the purpose of achieving and maintaining the dictatorship. The party is an instrument of the dictatorship of the proletariat.

"From this it follows that when classes disappear and the dictatorship of the proletariat withers away, the Party will also wither away."

13. QUESTION: **What is the true origin of the State and civil authority?**

ANSWER: a) Both arose from the necessity and desire of individuals to live as rational and social beings and to protect their lives and property from brute force. The family groups in all communities realized the need of uniting in clans, tribes and states in order to preserve their basic rights and common welfare, in order to be able to live together.

b) The State and civil authority exist for the benefit of all individual members of the community—for their common good. The individual does not exist for the State. Nor should he ever become a mere cog in the machinery of State power and control.

This authority of the State has its source in nature and has consequently God for its Author. This foundation of the State and the natural law is explained by Leo XIII in his Encyclical on the **Christian Constitution of States** and by St. Thomas Aquinas in his work on the **Governance of Rulers.**

14. QUESTION: **Under Communist theory, what is the actual purpose and function of the all-powerful State?**

ANSWER: In the present stage of history, the absolute State is a necessary instrument of authority, power, and guidance to direct the Communists of the world (themselves persuading wider groups of people by infiltration and the Communist line) to overthrow "capitalism" and bring about the World Soviet Dictatorship.

We must remind ourselves that in order to make this dictatorship palatable to those living under it, the Marxists promise that when the World Soviet Dictatorship is established this absolute State will "wither away" into the Communist or classless society.

15. QUESTION: **Has this objective of world rule been set down by any Communist leaders?**

ANSWER: It runs through all Communist discussion, the process for attaining the World Soviet Dictatorship being set down in detail in the **Program of the Communist International,** adopted at the Sixth World Congress of the Communist International in Moscow in 1928. The whole idea is well expressed by Joseph Stalin in his **Foundations of Leninism,** when he writes that the objective of the present period in Soviet history is "to consolidate the dictatorship of the proletariat in one country, using it as a base for the overthrow of imperialism in all countries. The revolution is spreading beyond the confines of one country; the period of world revolution has commenced."

16. QUESTION: **In order to forward its world-wide propaganda, how does the Soviet dictatorship describe itself?**

ANSWER: In the so-called Stalin Constitution, adopted in 1936 to pull the wool over the eyes of the United States, Article 1 says: "The Union of

Soviet Socialist Republics is a socialist state of workers and peasants."

As with most Communist phrases, this is the opposite of reality. The Soviet dictatorship is the iron rule over the workers and peasants and all other people. Soviet Russia and the "socialist countries" are ruled by Praesidiums (sometimes called Political Bureaus,) in the name of the Communist Parties who in turn act fictitiously in the name of the "democratic dictatorship." The real ruler is the the autocratic leader of the Communist Party of the Soviet Union, formerly Stalin, now Nikita Khrushchev.

At the Seventh World Congress of the Communist International, held in Moscow in 1935, Stalin was hailed by the delegates of all the Communist Parties of the world as "the leader, teacher, and guide of the proletariat and oppressed of the whole world."

17. QUESTION: **How do Communists regard all non-Soviet governments?**

ANSWER: As decadent forms of capitalist rule or "the bourgeois dictatorship." The term "imperialist nations" is often applied to the Western Powers by the Soviet leaders. As usual with Communist phraseology, this term is given a peculiar Communist meaning which will be examined later on and which arises from the significant volume, **Imperialism, the Highest Stage of Capitalism,** by V. I. Lenin.

In attacking the non-Soviet nations as "imperialist," however, the Soviet leaders not only keep alive the old grievances of colonial rule for Communist benefit, but also hide from full public scrutiny the imperialism which they are establishing under the guise of fighting imperialism. We shall see that this Communist tendency to attack the weaknesses or abuses of our present system in order to set up worse abuses along the same line is a peculiar feature of Marxism-Leninism.

18. QUESTION: **We can therefore say that the whole intent of Communist leadership in dealing with the free world, either by threats or by "smiles," is for the purpose of world domination?**

ANSWER: That is decidedly correct. Since the Communists will use any means, in accordance with their morality, to attain their ends, they will use war, or "peace," to attain world rule. Every "summit conference" is devised by Moscow for no other purpose than to weaken the democratic nations, to create division among them, and to advance Soviet conquest.

SUGGESTED READINGS:

The student should study carefully Chapter V and Chapter XIII of Father McFadden's **Philosophy of Communism,** dealing with Communism and the State.

Communist infiltration of the United States Government for subversive purposes is covered by numerous reports of the Senate Sub-Committee on Internal Security and House Committee on Un-American Activities, which can be consulted. Also it is the subject of a number of books, including the following:

Budenz, Louis F., **The Cry is Peace,** Henry Regnery Co., Chicago.

Chambers, Whittaker, **Witness,** Random House, New York.

de Toledano, Ralph, **Spies, Dupes, and Diplomats,** Duell, Sloan and Pearce, New York.

Concerning Soviet Russia, consult:

Dallin, David, **The Real Soviet Russia,** Yale University Press, New Haven, Conn.

Dallin, David and Nicolaevsky, Boris, **Forced Labor in Soviet Russia,** Yale University Press.

Djilas, Milovan, **The New Class,** Frederick A. Praeger, New York (to be read with caution, because of his social-democratic conclusions).

Leo XIII, **Great Encyclical Letters,** Benziger Brothers, New York: noting particularly pp. 107-134.

Pegis, Anton C., **Basic Writings of St. Thomas Aquinas,** Random House, N. Y.

CHAPTER IX

COMMUNISM AND THE WORKERS

1. QUESTION: **What part did the workers in Russia have in the 1917 Revolution?**

   ANSWER: The alleged "Workers' Revolution" of 1917 was not organized or dominated by labor groups or workingmen. It was planned and directed by international revolutionary forces, under the direction of what was to become the Communist Party. This Party and these revolutionary forces were led by V. I. Lenin (whose original name was Ulianov), the son of a district superintendent of schools who by reason of that fact was a member of the lower Great Russian nobility. Lenin was assisted prominently by Leon Trotsky (whose original name was Bernstein), also an intellectual. Neither one of these men was a worker, and that was the case with all their chief followers and leading supporters.

2. QUESTION: **How, then was the Russian revolution put over?**

   ANSWER: In a moment of chaos in World War I, the Bolsheviks (future Communists) seized power from the parliamentary revolutionary government of Alexander Kerensky, dissolving the constituent assembly by strong arm tactics. They then set up "the democratic dictatorship of the proletariat and peasantry," which was declared to be in reality the dictatorship of the proletariat only, but which was actually the dictatorship of the Communist Party.

3. QUESTION: **How did Lenin justify the Communist Party's acting as the guide and on behalf of the workers?**

ANSWER: In his work, **The Teachings of Karl Marx,** Lenin asserted (as Engels had before him) that Marxism flowed from the continuation and completion of "the three chief ideological currents of the Nineteenth Century." These are 1. German philosophy, centered around the writings of George F. W. Hegel and Ludwig Feuerbach; 2. French socialistic writings and "French revolutionary doctrines," especially as represented by Pierre J. Proudhon with his view that every historical period was characterized by a class war; 3. English economic theories, such as those of Adam Smith and David Ricardo, which Marx as usual turned in part against their authors.

Hence, the intellectuals, not the workers, contributed most to the origin and progress of Communism. Note how these three Western sources have become a scourge for the Western nations in the present century. Pope Pius XI outlined this well in the introduction to his Encyclical **Divini Redemptoris,** when he showed that the teachings of Communism arose from "the days when groups of 'intellectuals' were formed in an arrogant attempt to free civilization from the bonds of morality and religion."

From the over-simplification and artificial dove-tailing of these philosophical, economic, and socialistic teachings of the Nineteenth Century, Lenin on the basis of Marxist compilations, asserted that "the proletarian revolution" must be led by a chosen group, the Communist Party, which was to think for and guide the workers.

4. QUESTION: **Are not then these claims of a "dictatorship of the proletariat" and "the workers' revolution" a fraud?**

ANSWER: Yes, as with every other promise made by Marxism, the triumph of socialism turns these promises into their opposites. Under the alleged "dictatorship of the proletariat" collective bargaining has been abolished, strikes are illegal and criminal, and the so-called trade unions have become merely production-producing machines.

In a similar manner, Lenin's revolutionary cry "Land to the Peasants," which also characterized the 1917 Revolution, was transformed into the turning of all land into the property of the Soviet State.

5. QUESTION: **When the Communists speak of "the rule of the proletariat" they therefore mean actually "the rule of the Communist Party?"**

ANSWER: That is decidedly correct. The Communists envision themselves as a comparatively small group of "social scientists," the sole possessors of the secrets of Marxism-Leninism. They are to lead and guide the workers in the revolution. Consequently, it is they (under the leadership of Moscow) who know what is best for the people of the world, according to their view, and by infiltration and finally the stimulation of force are to establish the Party's rule over the world.

6. QUESTION: **Was this conception that the Party is actually to act for the subservient "working class" brought out clearly in the writings of Lenin and his successors?**

ANSWER: That is correct. The whole emphasis of Lenin's writings—notably in **What Is To Be Done** and in **One Step Forward, Two Steps Backward**—was for the creation of a small and disciplined group which would become "the vanguard" and directing power, acting in the name of "the working class."

The summary of Lenin's views can be read in Joseph V. Stalin's **Foundations of Leninism.** In the chapter on "The Party," Stalin brings out the six necessary features of the "revolutionary party, bold enough to lead the proletarians to the struggle for power," on the basis of Lenin's writings. The very first of these features is that "the Party is the vanguard of the working class." It is thereby characterized as "the general staff of the proletariat in the class war."

7. QUESTION: **Is this arrogant idea of the Communist Party as the depository of wisdom for "the workers" clearly set forth by Lenin and Stalin?**

ANSWER: The best way to show how the matter is presented is to quote from Stalin's own words, he in turn drawing on Lenin's declarations. In speaking of the Party as the "vanguard" for the proletariat, Stalin says that it is the only force that can "give correct guidance to the proletarian millions," who are incapable of thinking for themselves.

Then he clearly declares: "No army at war can dispense with an experienced General Staff if it does not want to court certain defeat. Is it not clear that the proletariat can still less dispense with such a General Staff if it does not want to give itself up to be devoured by its mortal enemies? But where is this General Staff? Only the revolutionary party of the proletariat can serve as this General Staff. The working class without a revolutionary party is an army without a General Staff. The Party is the General Staff of the proletariat."

8. QUESTION: **When the Communist leaders or followers refer to their Party as "the Party of the proletariat" or "the advance guard of the working class," are they not using these terms in an artificial sense?**

ANSWER: That is exactly what they are doing. The "proletariat" of which Karl Marx wrote was predicted by him to become more and more depressed and poverty stricken. This followed from his theory of "surplus value" under which the workers were supposedly robbed of several hours of labor a day and under "the capitalist law of accumulation," which led to this increasing depression of the workers' conditions. Such has not occurred in the modern world, specifically in the United States of America.

The "proletariat" of Lenin and Stalin is equally artificial in that, as we have seen, the "dictatorship of the proletariat" is actually the dictatorship of the Communist Party, and that in turn is actually the dictatorship of the Master of the Kremlin.

9. QUESTION: **How and why did so many workers in Russia and Europe eventually join in the Marxist revolutionary movement?**

ANSWER: It professed to be a true, universal movement for the benefit of the workers, to end capitalistic exploitation and to transfer wealth and political power from the middle and upper classes to the working classes. The slogan: "Workers of the world, unite," has been a popular, effective appeal. This final slogan of the **Communist Manifesto** is still considered so potent that it appears prominently on the front cover of each issue, even today, of the **World Marxist Review**, official directive-giver to the comrades of the world.

10. QUESTION: **Despite these alluring promises made by the Communists to the workers, can it be said that the Communist Party has ever had the adherence of the majority of the workers in any country taken over by Soviet Power?**

ANSWER: At no time has the majority of workers in any country been adherent to the Communist Party. Even in Czechoslovakia where the Communist Party grew rapidly after the Red Army came in 1945, the Party never obtained a majority of votes for the Czech parliament and did not have the adherence of the majority of the workers. Soviet rule has always been imposed by force over every conquered people, after the country to be conquered has been undermined by Communist infiltration of government, press, and other agencies.

11. QUESTION: **What is the promise made by Communism to the workers, in fact, to all the people, of the so-called colonial countries?**

ANSWER: Lenin was shrewd enough to foresee that the colonial and colored peoples would eventually strive for and attain independence. And he brought out the view that "imperialism" represented a higher and last stage of capitalism. In this stage, it was essential to "monopoly capital" to exploit wider and wider groups of colonies. At the same time, particularly through Stalin's development of Lenin's teachings represented in his section on the National Question in **Foundations of Leninism** and his noted book **Marxism and the National and Colonial Question,** it was brought out that the only real road to "liberation" of these colonial peoples including the colonial workers, was under subservience to the dictatorship of the proletariat. Thus, in allegedly fighting "imperialism," the Communists by means of Soviet Russia and now Red China began to establish an imperialism of their own, directed toward taking over the world.

12. QUESTION: **When the Communists use the terms "imperialism" and "imperialist countries" as they do repeatedly, they have a different meaning in mind from what we do when we use those terms?**

ANSWER: That is correct. By "imperialism" the Communists never mean the Soviet taking-over

by force of various countries. That is always
"liberation." The "imperialist countries" are
always the democratic nations.

13. QUESTION: **Because of this view that "liberation" can
come to the colonial peoples finally only
through "the dictatorship of the proletariat,"
the Communists must necessarily establish a
slave labor system for these so-called colonial peoples when Soviet Power is established
over them?**

ANSWER: That is precisely what takes place. This is
now being manifested most strongly in the
case of the "peoples' Communes" of Red
China, in which the workers and peasants
are reduced to the most degrading conditions and a determined effort is made to
destroy the family. In Soviet Russia, itself,
and in all the other "socialist countries," this
is also manifested by the denial of the right
to organize to the workers and the fact that
their alleged trade unions must merely be
echoes of the Communist line as set down by
Moscow.

14. QUESTION: **Has the history of Communist infiltration into the trade unions of America demonstrated
that these Communists are not interested in
the welfare of the workers or in the trade
unions, but merely in advancing the Communist line?**

ANSWER: That is what the history of Communist relations to the unions here would show beyond
doubt and which caused the CIO in 1950 so
severely to reprimand the Communist Party.

COMMUNISM AND THE WORKERS

15. QUESTION: **Can you give some of the high lights of that history?**

ANSWER: In 1922, the Trade Union Educational League headed by William Z. Foster, who had just become a Communist, became a section of the "Red International of Labor Unions," operated from Moscow. The purpose of the TUEL, as Foster admits, was at that time to infiltrate the regular labor movement as Lenin had just recommended in his **Left Wing Communism—An Infantile Disorder.**

Then, in 1929, this TUEL became the Trade Union Unity League, an alleged center for separate Red trade unions. This was in line with the decisions of the Sixth World Congress of the Communist International, held in Moscow in 1928.

In 1935, the TUEL was dissolved, and all the Red unions went first into the American Federation of Labor unions and then one year later all tumbled out of the AF of L into the CIO. These acts were in accordance with the Seventh World Congress of the Communist International, held in Moscow in 1935. This was the so-called "United Front Congress," which brought forth the "Trojan Horse" tactic of wide infiltration of government, press, business, and labor.

When Moscow opened the Cold War against the United States, the Communists took such a stand against this country and for Soviet Russia in the CIO that they were expelled.

In 1959 the Supreme Court decisions rescued the Communist Party from its previous difficulties, as all Communist publications proclaimed, and the followers of Moscow planned re-infiltration of the regular labor movement. They did this in widespread discussions in **Political Affairs,** theoretical organ of the Communist Party.

16. QUESTION: **What is the attitude of the American trade union movement as a whole toward Communism?**

Answer: As the visit of Dictator Nikita Khrushchev to this country in 1959 demonstrated, the AFL-CIO is officially opposed to Communism and to the advance of the Communist line, when the labor leaders know what this line is. This was dramatized by the action of the Executive Council of the AFL-CIO, under the leadership of President George Meany, in refusing to see Khrushchev because of his suppression of trade unions.

While some AFL-CIO leaders, notably Walter Reuther and James Carey, did see Khrushchev and talked with him, the embarrassing questions they asked so angered him that he became abusive. Later, the Kremlin engaged in a bitter attack on Reuther, as usual of a degrading personal nature.

17. QUESTION: **What is the greatest weakness of American labor leadership in these stands against Communism?**

ANSWER: While American labor leadership has shown in the Khrushchev incidents much more courage in opposing Communism than many sections in the Big Business world, there is one danger that stands out which may lead to new widespread infiltration by the Communists. That is the tendency of certain labor leaders, in order to cultivate a "liberal" reputation, to go along with the Communist line, not always recognizing it as such. This has led time and time again to the Communists sneaking into the trade unions on the basis of allegedly agreeing with certain labor leaders who are non-Communists but who did follow the Communist line, as for instance, in "the battle against McCarthyism," which we shall later see was concocted by the Communists to bring America to its knees before the Kremlin.

CHAPTER X

COMMUNISM IN THE UNITED STATES

1. QUESTION: **What has been the role of the Communist Party in the United States?**

   ANSWER: It has been well described in the book, **Masters of Deceit**: "The Communist Party, USA, has been and is engaged in an all-out war against American freedom. Its tactics of confusion, retreat, advance, infiltration, and hypocrisy are in full play. The attack is both legal and illegal, offensive and defensive, open and concealed.

   "Above the surface a gigantic propaganda and agitation campaign is in progress, a campaign that depends for success upon the support of non-communists. Basic communist stategy dictates that non-communist hands, knowingly or unknowingly, under communist guidance, must further the influence of the communist world." (Ch. 14, p. 195.)

2. QUESTION: **Have Communists in the United States been able to manipulate the thinking and actions of non-Communists on a wide scale?**

   ANSWER: That has been the secret of their success in conquering as much of the world as they have today—their ability to persuade non-Communists in the United States to take the stand originated in Moscow.

3. QUESTION: **Is this done largely by the agency of Communist fronts?**

ANSWER: To a marked degree by Communist fronts but not entirely. The role of the front, partly put in the background by the Communists for the present moment but giving a clue to more subtle infiltration, can be described thus:

A front is an organization which the communists openly or secretly control. The communists realize that they are not welcome in American society. Party influence, therefore, is transmitted, time after time, by a belt of concealed members, sympathizers, and dupes. Fronts become transmission belts between the Party and the non-communist world. Earl Browder, when head of the Party, said that transmission belts mean having Communists work among the masses in the various organizations.

4. QUESTION: **Can we feel the impact of past Communist fronts even at the present day?**

ANSWER: Since the Communists originally organized fronts in almost every conceivable field—to advance the Communist line in press, radio, television, in labor and business, education and the Government—their impact on American thinking and action has been very great. Two examples can be given of many in our history. Today, the United States has thrown off most of its real guard against Soviet Communism, because of Nikita Khrushchev's world-wide false and fraudulent "peace" campaign. If the reader were to consult the excellent report of the House Committee on Un-American Activities for April 1, 1951, entitled **The Communist Peace Offensive: The Attempt to Disarm and Defeat America,** he would see that our country had been drenched with Moscow-made propaganda along this line. Even in that early day, there functioned front after front, designed to "soften us up" on the question of "peace," thus slowing us down to Soviet Russia's advantage.

The next example is the constant battle of the Communists for "civil liberties." In this campaign, they have falsely represented that if the Communists are curbed in any way in their seditious activities, other sections of the American people will have their own freedom curtailed.

5. QUESTION: **Has this campaign for "freedom" for the Communists to carry on their subversive activities been as successful in the USA as their "peace" crusade?**

ANSWER: It has been so successful that repeated decisions by the United States Supreme Court now render the Government of the United States and of the several states impotent to act against the Communist conspiracy within our borders. Lately, as the result of public alarm, protests from patriotic American groups and the report by the American Bar Association critical of the Supreme Court have had some effect. While this has led to some of the Supreme Court's pro-Communist decisions being slightly reversed or modified, the change is so small that the

Communists can rejoice in the present "atmosphere."

6. QUESTION: **Is the extent of Communist infiltration into our life and thinking to be judged solely by Communist fronts?**

ANSWER: Most decidedly not. At all times, there were also the secret cells in organizations which in themselves were non-Communist, at least originally so. Since the Sixteenth National Convention in February, 1957, the Communist Party for the moment has returned much more to this form of making America do what it wants it to do than before. Partly, this action was taken because of the extensive expose of the personnel of the Communist fronts by the Congressional committees in what the Communists call "the period of McCarthyism."

7. QUESTION: **The strength of the Communist Party, as a consequence, is not to be measured by the number of its members but the extent of its infiltration?**

ANSWER: That is correct. While of course the Communists want to enlarge their parties, particularly in non-Soviet countries, in order to increase the possibilities of infiltration and espionage, that is not paramount. The first thing is that the Party be well disciplined and in complete subservience to Moscow.

It is clear that one representative in the State Department, helping to direct the Yalta policy and other policies, was more important to the Kremlin than thousands of Communists would be. It is evident that the entire "Washington cell," which affected

American policy in a pro-Soviet direction by its penetration of our Government, was more vital to Moscow than hordes of Communists not well organized would be.

8. QUESTION: **How can we distinguish the penetration of our Government, press, television, or other agencies by the Communists?**

ANSWER: We can acquaint ourselves, of course, with the valuable reports of the Congressional committees exposing concealed Communists and giving lists of Communist fronters. But our main object as a private citizen must be to know the Communist line. Anyone forwarding that line, which always originates in Moscow, is injuring America. It makes no difference whether he is a veteran Communist, a fellow-traveler conscious of what he is doing, or merely a dupe.

9. QUESTION: **Can you give examples of the triumph of the Communist line, as dictated by Moscow, in American thinking?**

ANSWER: There are too many examples to repeat them all here. There is the whole first period of American retreat before Soviet Power, opening with our recognition of Soviet Russia in 1933 and followed by the taking over of all the countries behind the iron curtain by Soviet Power. In each one of these cases. as many books by leading authorities have shown, these countries were betrayed into Soviet hands by the cooperation and eager acquiescence of the United States.

Unless we are much more on guard than is the case at the present moment, we are now at a period of complete confusion dating from the visit of Dictator Khrushchev to the United States.

10. QUESTION: **Did the formal recognition of the Soviet regime by the United States Government in 1933 notably further the "Red Revolution?"**

ANSWER: Yes, in several important ways. When the late President Franklin D. Roosevelt formally recognized the Soviet Regime in 1933, contrary to the advice of many American statesmen, Communism was given undeserved respectability in the eyes of the world; the power of the Soviet tyrants over their own people was increased; and diplomatic relations between Soviet Russia and the United States became a serious threat to World Peace and Freedom.

11. QUESTION: **How was this serious threat manifested?**

ANSWER: Marxist spies and secret agents came unmolested into the United States, and every Soviet Legation, Consulate, and Trade Bureau became an anti-American spy-ring; the Communist underground and above-ground conspiracy was promoted with little or no hindrance; Red agents, driven from Spain and France after the Spanish Revolution, were brought here under government auspices. Many of them have remained here ever since to aid in the overthrow of the United States.

In addition, there was the more important development of the extensive infiltration of our Government by concealed Communists and their appeasement friends. This resulted in the adoption of those disastrous policies which led to the betrayal of China, Poland,

Hungary, and all the rest of the present "iron curtain" countries.

12. QUESTION: **Is infiltration of our Government the sole method employed by the Communists to attain these ends?**

ANSWER: No; in each case, the ground is first prepared by creating "the proper favorable atmosphere" to which the Communist paper, **The Worker,** frequently refers. This "atmosphere" is brought about by infiltration of sections of our press, radio, television, and other sources of information.

13. QUESTION: **But did not Soviet Russia solemnly promise to end Communist activities within the United States as the result of the Pact of Recognition in 1933?**

ANSWER: Yes, and that proved to be a sample of Soviet perfidy which should have taught us long ago not to be the continual victims of internal appeasement and the Communist line which we have proved to be. In the Pact itself, in return for recognition, Soviet Russia solemnly promised to end subversive activities in the United States. Not only did they not do so, but they intensified this penetration of our Government and other agencies.

14. QUESTION: **Did the United States Government take action on this obvious perfidy?**

ANSWER: To an extent. In 1935, the Seventh World Congress of the Communist International convened in Moscow, with American Communists present as faithful servants of the Kremlin. Secretary of State Cordell Hull, with the consent of President Roosevelt, protested against this obvious meeting to create subversion in the United States. But the Soviet Government answered that it was no more interested in meetings of the Communist International than the United States would be in a meeting of the United States Chamber of Commerce. This cynical reply was accepted by us as another token of surrender to the Communist line.

15. QUESTION: **With this example of Soviet perfidy, intensified by the period of the Hitler-Stalin Alliance, what did we do after World War II?**

ANSWER: Under the Moscow slogan that "friendly nations were required on the Soviet borders in order to ensure peace," we proceeded to betray all the nations behind the iron curtain. The result was not peace but a widening of the possibilities of war or slavery or both.

16. QUESTION: **Is there official evidence that large numbers of Soviet agents actually penetrated many of the U. S. Federal Government agencies?**

ANSWER: The official evidence is abundant and includes the sordid un-American activities of Soviet or pro-Soviet agents.

The various Senate and House investigations have revealed "wholesale" subversive activity on an incredible scale among Federal employees, many of them holding key positions in our government. The testimony fills several volumes, and the facts have been printed in several issues of the Congressional reports of committees of the Senate and House, notably the report of the Committee on Internal Security concerning the Institute of Pacific Relations.

As one instance, it can be said that in his recent biography on page 453, General Patrick Hurley states: "A total of 833 persons had been dismissed from the State Department (by 1948) for subversive activity." All these were dismissed only because of pressure, largely from Congressional committees. Today, although the Government to some extent may still be penetrated in this fashion, there has been a let-down on any attempted examination of the subversive elements that may still be embedded there.

17. QUESTION: **Can you give another outstanding example of the triumph of the Communist line in American thought and action?**

ANSWER: This is particularly exemplified in the "battle against McCarthyism," which was concocted by the Communists and became completely dominant in American thinking and action. The "battle against McCarthyism" was originated in the March, 1950, special session of the national committee of the Communist Party. This is reported for the benefit of the comrades in the May, 1950, issue of **Political Affairs.** The "battle" was ordered to begin by Gus Hall, later a fugitive of justice from the United States after being convicted of plotting for the violent overthrow of this Government. In the March session of the Communist national committee, Hall opened the campaign against "McCarthyism" when he declared that the McCarthys must be put into the un-American, subversive garbage heap where they belong." It was the orders of this Moscow agent and convicted proponent of the violent overthrow of the United States Government which helped to rule American thought.

18. QUESTION: **Can you briefly outline the further progress of "the battle against McCarthyism?"**

ANSWER: For a short time, Hall's orders did not take on full steam. But in October, 1952, Joseph Stalin intervened and ordered the comrades "of the imperialist nations" to raise higher "the banner of bourgeois civil liberties."

This order was printed in **Political Affairs** for October, 1952. It led to a new upsurge of "the battle against McCarthyism."

By June 1, 1953, the **Daily Worker** could report in a leading editorial, "Our Crusade Hits Home," that it was making tremendous progress in this battle. Many conservative organizations were following the Communist lead, it said, citing many of them. In the same month—June, 1953—**Political Affairs,** official theoretical organ of the Communist Party, ran an important article "The Anatomy of McCarthyism." In that important directive article, it was declared that this battle was not against an individual alone but against all those who would seek to declare the Communist Party in the United States a "conspiracy." So successful has this campaign been, that the United States today cannot do much against the Communist conspiracy in its midst, due to the Supreme Court decisions which have been criticized by the American Bar Association.

Character !

19. QUESTION: **Have we evidences today of the triumph of the Communist line within the United States?**

ANSWER: The whole recent history of the United States is a record of the triumph of the Communist line, adopted partially and reluctantly but to too great a degree.

In 1955, we went to the summit meeting at Geneva, because of Soviet pressure in the countries which have Communist Parties and because of the appeasement forces in the United States. This represented another defeat. While we were endlessly debating at Geneva with Soviet representatives, they were making their great break-through in the Middle East, now represented particularly by predominant Communist influence in Iraq.

20. QUESTION: **Was this followed up by further advances of the Communist line?**

ANSWER: Many of the orders given by Nikita Khrushchev at the 20th Congress of the Communist Party of the Soviet Union in February, 1956, have been obeyed by the United States Government. One of these immediately is cultural exchanges, which Khrushchev recommended in order to be able to create a spirit of complacency in this country and to plant Soviet agents here. Another is the sweeping victory of the idea of "peaceful coexistence," specifically represented by our servile and warm reception of Khrushchev in this country.

21. QUESTION: **Can you give one example of how our "invitation" to Dictator Khrushchev built up Soviet Power against the United States?**

ANSWER: We could give many, but will restrict ourselves to one. In connection with the Khrushchev visit, the Communist press has been busy throughout the eighty-three countries in which Communist parties function in telling in effect the comrades that the American nation agrees with Soviet actions.

In Number 37 of the **New Times** from Moscow, (one of the issues of September, 1959) great emphasis is placed on the fact that Khrushchev's trip was signalized by his article "On Peaceful Coexistence" in the American magazine, **Foreign Affairs**. And it is further emphasized that the Soviet dictator wrote in that article:

"Apart from the commitment of non-aggression, it (peaceful coexistence) also presupposes an obligation on the part of all states to desist from violating each other's territorial integrity and sovereignty in any form and under any pretext whatsoever."

By publishing such crass nonsense as this—in view of the Soviet conquest by force of the Baltic and Balkan countries, of Hungary and Asian nations—a leading American magazine helps the Soviet cause. It permits the Soviet propagandists to sneak into the press of the rest of the free world the idea that the United States actually approves of the slaughter of the Hungarian people and of other Soviet conquests.

22. QUESTION: **How, then, can we proceed to move in the direction of saving America?**

ANSWER: By finding ways and means of letting our

representatives, press, and other agencies know the following:

1. That of its very nature, Soviet Communism cannot be dealt with in summit conferences, because it will not proceed to such meetings in good faith. That we cannot, because of the nature of Communism, fall victims to "peaceful coexistence," Khrushchev visits, or "cultural exchanges"

2. That we must be aware at all times of the Communist line, knowing at the present moment that it is intended to lull us to sleep. Meanwhile, the Kremlin will go forward with its policy of revolutions in Latin America, Southeast Asia, and the Middle East.

3. That we must distinguish between Communism and reforms, knowing that while we oppose the Kremlin's purposes and line, we also zealously forward the legitimate interests of the trade union movement, the rights of the Negro people, and opposition to anti-Semitism.

SUGGESTED READINGS:

For the Skeptic: Selected Readings on Communist Activity in the United States of America. Edited by Lyle H. Munson. The Bookmailer, Inc., N. Y.

Masters of Deceit. J. Edgar Hoover, Henry Holt, New York.

I Saw Poland Betrayed. Arthur Bliss Lane. (former U. S. Ambassador to Poland.) Bobbs Merrill, Indianapolis.

The Communist Party Vs. the CIO. Max M. Kampelman. Praeger, New York (despite certain confusing "liberal" weaknesses).

America's Second Crusade. William Henry Chamberlin. Henry Regnery, Chicago.

Communism Vs. the Negro. William A. Nolan. Henry Regnery, Chicago.

Particularly do we recommend the reports of the House Committee on Un-American Activities and the Senate Committee on Internal Security, which contain invaluable information.

CHAPTER XI

COMMUNISM AND CHINA

1. QUESTION: **Is the Communist conquest of China due principally to Soviet influence?**

ANSWER: Yes, to Soviet influence and trickery, accompanied eventually by American betrayal of the Chinese people into Soviet hands. As early as July, 1912, five years before the Bolshevik **coup d'etat** in Russia, Lenin had published articles on Dr. Sun Yat-sen's agitation for democracy in China, and had concerned himself with how to turn the coming "democratic revolution" there finally into a "proletarian revolution."

Immediately after the "Bolshevik Revolution" in Russia, Moscow began to interfere in the internal affairs of China. As Chiang Kai-shek states in the opening of his remarkable book, **Soviet Russia in China:** "Moscow's China policy was a double-faced one. On the one hand, the Soviet Foreign Office carried on diplomatic negotiations with the Chinese Government. On the other, the Communist International proceeded to set up a Chinese Communist Party."

2. QUESTION: **The Chinese Communist Party was therefore a Soviet creation?**

ANSWER: Most necessarily. Being dedicated to the world Soviet revolution, the Moscow dictatorship took an intense interest in furthering Communist conquest of China. As Chiang Kai-shek again says: "The Chinese Communist Party is not indigenous to China. It is an outgrowth of Soviet Russia and the Communist empire."

This assertion is supported by the history of Soviet relations with China, the maneuvers of Michael Borodin as the representative of the Communist International in China, and the "united fronts" of the Chinese Communists with the organization founded by Dr. Sun Yat-sen, the Kuomintang. All of these moves from 1922 on were for the purpose of erasing any democratic revolution in China by turning it into a Moscow-led Communist conquest.

3. QUESTION: **Is this view of the Soviet creation of Communist China confirmed by statements of the Chinese Communist leaders to the comrades of the world?**

ANSWER: Yes, repeated over and over again, the statements of the Chinese Communist leaders have always acknowledged their inspiration to Soviet Russia. As a recent instance there is the leading article in the October, 1959, issue of the **World Marxist Review,** contributed by Liu Shao-chi on "The Triumph of Marxism-Leninism in China." The author is the successor of Mao Tse-tung as "President" of Red China and one of the leading theoreticians of the Communist conspiracy. In the very beginning of his article, which is concerned with the tenth anniversary of "the Chinese People's Republic," Liu Shao-chi declared: "The Chinese revolution is the continuation of the Great October Socialist Revolution (in Soviet Russia) which opened a new era in the history of mankind and initiated the process of changing the world."

4. QUESTION: **Do the Chinese Communists when speaking to themselves and to the comrades of the world continue to acknowledge the leadership of Moscow?**

   ANSWER: They do this repeatedly and almost monotonously. In his speech at the opening of the Tenth Anniversary Celebration, Liu Shao-chi referred emphatically to "the countries of the socialist camp headed by the Soviet Union." (This speech appears as a supplement to the **Peking Review** of October 1, 1959.)

5. QUESTION: **Moscow's plans for the conquest of China were long prepared and carefully mapped out?**

   ANSWER: That is correct. In the final work that he wrote, just before his death, Lenin stressed the importance of the "victory of socialism" in Asia. In this work, **Better Fewer, But Better,** the Soviet dictator asserted that "in the last analysis, the outcome of the struggle will be determined by the fact that Russia, India, China, etc., constitute the overwhelming majority of the population of the globe." Their going Communist would assure "the final victory of Socialism!"
   (This appears in V. I. Lenin's **Selected Works,** V. IX, p. 387 ff.)

6. QUESTION: **Were these final words of Lenin set down in an official program of action by the interna-**

tional communist conspiracy in regard to China?

ANSWER: At the Sixth World Congress of the Communist International, held in Moscow in 1928, a number of "theses" were adopted for the specific furtherance of world revolution. (This was the first world congress which was completely dominated by Joseph V. Stalin.) Among these "theses" was a very important document entitled: "Theses on the Revolutionary Movement in the Colonies and Semi-Colonies." This was a detailed plan, covering many pages, of how the democratic yearnings of the people of China, India, and similar colonial countries could be transformed by Communist tactics into the victory of the Soviet dictatorship in those countries.

(Photo-offset copy of this document, reproducing its publication in **International Press Correspondence** for December 12, 1928 can be obtained free from the American China Policy Association, 1 West 37th St., New York, 10, N. Y.)

7. QUESTION: **What was the chief task laid down by this congress?**

ANSWER: "The building up and development of the Communist Parties in the colonies and semi-colonies," including specifically China. These parties were to make use of the democratic desires of the people to achieve the proletarian dictatorship and in the process to inculcate hatred of "the imperialist nations." (These were and are the democratic nations.)

In an additional "manifesto" to "the workers of the world" and to "all oppressed colonial peoples," the Sixth World Congress of the Communist International directed particular hatred at "the transatlantic vampire, the United States." This is a conception frequently repeated and now indelibly embedded in Communist consciousness and in that of Communist sympathizers throughout the Far East and the world as a whole.

8. QUESTION: **Did certain American forces, interests, and individuals cooperate in betraying the Chinese people into Communist hands and in thus achieving these Moscow goals?**

   ANSWER: That is precisely what happened. Concealed Communists, fellow travelers, and appeasers in the United States persuaded our government to pursue a policy which cooperated in the Soviet conquest of China. As one instance of many, there appeared in the July 4, 1943 issue of **Far Eastern Survey,** official publication of the notorious Institute of Pacific Relations, an article by an "expert," T. A. Bisson. It was said there that there were two Chinas, a "democratic China," that portion under Communist control, and a "feudalistic China," meaning the Republic of China under Chiang Kai-shek.

   It was "expert advice" of this character which the Senate Sub-Committee on Internal Security, under the late Senator Pat McCarran, found to have decided United States policy in aiding Soviet Russia in China.

9. QUESTION: **What was the method taken by these so-called "Far Eastern experts" in newspapers,**

magazines, books, and in the Government to deceive the American people on China?

ANSWER: They fraudulently represented the Chinese Communists to be the leaders in "a national, independent agrarian reform movement," not organically linked up with Moscow and not Communist in the real sense of the word. This whole school of "Far Eastern experts" betrayed the United States into a policy which led to the loss of China into Soviet hands and the bringing about of the bloody war in Korea. All of this stands revealed in the hearings and reports of the Senate Sub-Committee on Internal Security into the Institute of Pacific Relations, which proved to be the chief agency for infiltrating pro-Communist ideas into the State Department and other branches of the Government.

10. QUESTION: Did the American Communists encourage the appeasers, both as writers for the Chinese Communists and as activists in the State Department?

ANSWER: They did most emphatically. As an instance, we have the account in the **Daily Worker** written by Joseph Starobin, its foreign editor, reviewing Philip Jaffe's **New Frontiers in Asia.** He took that occasion to praise many of those writers on the Far East who were deceiving Americans concerning the nature of the Reds in China. Jaffe, it should be recalled, is the Soviet agent who accompanied Owen Lattimore on a special trip to the Red-ruled provinces of China in 1937 and who directed the stealing of 1700 confidential documents on China from the State Department and other American Government agencies in the **Amerasia case.**

11. QUESTION: **Of the writers applauded on that occasion by the Communists, what did Starobin say?**

ANSWER: "Militarists like Patrick J. Hurley are riled by the virtual unanimity of American intellectual opinion on the broad issues of the future of Asia. The writers, experts, journalists— even career diplomats in the State Department—are almost unanimous in their judgment of the reactionary character of the Kuomintang leaders, in their sympathy for the Chinese Communist program, and their emphasis on the need of an independent, democratic India. There is probably no other phase of American policy on which there is such a broad agreement among well-informed people. This has given rise to a virtual renaissance of American writing and thinking on the Far East."

Starobin went on to heap praise upon Owen Lattimore, Kate Mitchell, Lawrence K. Rosinger, Andrew Roth, Harrison Forman, and Gunther Stein.

(See Budenz, **The Cry Is Peace,** pp. 45, 46.)

12. QUESTION: **Is this the full list of the writers and activists who are plugging for the Chinese Communists in America?**

ANSWER: It is only a beginning. As one instance, we find prominent writers portraying the Chinese Communists as "agrarian reformers," in the pages of our largest and most representative national weeklies. Those who wanted to write critical books or articles on the Reds in China did not receive a welcome from leading publishers, and as one ex-Communist put it, "a little iron curtain" was drawn down on American thinking.

13. QUESTION: **Can you designate just who a few of these champions of the Reds in China were?**

ANSWER: Owen Lattimore functioned as an editor for the Institute for Pacific Relations, then as a special adviser to the White House and the State Department on China and the Far East. After extensive hearings, the Senate Sub-Committee on Internal Security in its special report declared Lattimore to be "a conscious, articulate instrument of the Soviet conspiracy." It also declared that "Owen Lattimore and John Carter Vincent were instrumental in bringing about a change in the United States policy in 1945 favorable to the Chinese Communists." This was a devastating judgment on the man who had been called by Washington "our leading Far East expert."

John Carter Vincent, mentioned by the Senate Sub-Committee with Lattimore, was not a writer but had represented our Government for a number of years in the Far East, being formerly in charge of the Far Eastern section of the State Department. Of him the Senate Sub-Committee also said: "Over a period of years, John Carter Vincent was the principal fulcrum of IPR pressures and influence in the State Department." The IPR stands for the Institute of Pacific Relations, of which the committee said: "The IPR has been considered by the American Communist Party and by Soviet officials as an instrument of Communist policy, propaganda, and military intelligence ... members of the small core of officials and staff members who controlled IPR were either Communists or pro-Communists."

14. QUESTION: **Were there any Soviet espionage agents among these writers, of the same character as Alger Hiss in the State Department and Harry Dexter White in the Treasury Department?**

ANSWER: Testimony before the Senate Sub-Committee on Internal Security revealed that at least Israel Epstein, Gunther Stein, and Agnes Smedley were Soviet espionage agents. A prominent writer for the IPR, Epstein, is now working for the Red Government of Communist China.

15. QUESTION: **Did these writings and intrigues of Communists and friends of Communists in America have any immediate effect on our personnel in China?**

ANSWER: It affected General Joseph Stilwell and made him decidedly pro-Communist in China and hostile to Generalissimo Chiang Kai-shek. On the other hand, when General Albert C. Wedemeyer succeeded Stilwell, recognized the trickery of the Communists, and began to follow a truly democratic policy, he was removed from his post.

16. QUESTION: **Did these writings and intrigues in favor of the Chinese Communists also affect the United States policy?**

ANSWER: They affected our policies in such a way that the United States proceeded to betray the

Republic of China and to build up the power of the Chinese Communists. This was done in so many ways that they cannot all be reviewed here. Prominent among them were:

a. Despite our previous pledge to Chiang Kai-shek at the Cairo Conference, that the United States would maintain the integrity of the Republic of China, we completely retracted that pledge at Yalta in effect. This second conference of the Big Three, held in February, 1945, turned over the rich Chinese province of Manchuria to Soviet Russia and made grants of the Port of Darien and Port Arthur which helped to make Soviet Russia eventually, working with the Chinese Communists, the master of China. William Henry Chamberlin, the noted authority on Soviet Affairs, has termed the Yalta agreement "the Munich called Yalta."

b. All through the subsequent maneuvers of the Chinese Communists against Chiang Kai-shek, the United States brought pressure on the Republic of China to enter into protracted conferences with the Communists. In each instance, the Reds used the breathing spells to get the Japanese arms from Soviet Russia out of Manchuria into their hands and to recruit the troops to man those guns.

c. From Yalta on, as a matter of fact, the United States pursued a policy of constantly yielding to Soviet pressures until we actually tripped up Chiang Kai-shek and insured Communist victory on the Chinese mainland.

17. QUESTION: **In addition to John Carter Vincent, were there other concealed Communists or sympathizers with the Communists or followers of the Communist line in our diplomatic service in China?**

ANSWER: There were, and their presence in China was one of the most important factors in the Communist victory. The Senate Sub-Committee on Internal Security designated many as following a pro-Communist policy, naming specifically among others John Stewart Service, Solomon Adler, and John Patton Davies. There were also scores of subordinates of the State Department who adhered to the IPR policy.

(Statements to this effect appear in testimony at the hearings before the Senate Committee on Armed Forces and the Committee on Foreign Relations—the MacArthur inquiry—June 4, 1951. They are also explained at great length by General Patrick J. Hurley in his biography written by Don Lohbeck, published in 1956.)

18. QUESTION: **What did the Communists proceed to do in regard to religion after they seized power in China?**

ANSWER: As happens whenever the Marxists are in power, the Christian religion has been marked for "liquidation," which means extinction. Skillful changes of tactics have been used by the Communists in order to wipe out both Catholics and Protestants. There were carried out huge hysterical campaigns against "the foreigners," making the missionaries from non-Communist lands the butt of this persecution. In this reign of terror it was that Bishop Francis Xavier Ford was martyred. Jailing missionaries, forcing them to live under the most brutal conditions, attempting by every vile means to extort "confessions" from them, the Reds were able by death or exile to get rid of most of the "foreign" missionaries, both Catholic and Protestant.

19. QUESTION: **Did they follow up this persecution with new tactics designed to liquidate religion?**

ANSWER: Having got rid of the "foreign" missionaries, the Reds changed their tactics once more and sought to bring about what amounts to Communist control of the Churches. Thus, among the Catholics, they formed "patriotic" associations, which led to the schism away from the Vatican. The aim of this schism is to break Chinese Catholics away from any contact with the Papacy and to make them completely subservient to the Red rulers. Similar procedure is being carried on against Protestants.

20. QUESTION: **What is supposedly "the great achievement" of the Chinese Communists to date?**

ANSWER: It is "the great leap forward" which was adopted in 1956, in accordance with the Marxist concept of dialectical materialism that in certain stages of history there must be a violent leap. This "great leap forward" concentrated on the development of heavy industries and neglected the living conditions of the people. It was also accompanied by the enforcement of "voluntary labor" upon intellectuals, so that they were obliged to go out into the farm country to engage in the building of big projects or in other enterprises requiring manual labor. The "great leap forward" was crowned from the Communist viewpoint by the establishment in 1958 of the "Peoples' Communes."

21. QUESTION: **What are these "Peoples' Communes" and how do they work?**

ANSWER: There have been many studies made of the alleged "Peoples' Communes" which show, even by Communist admissions, that they bring about a barrack-like existence among a great portion of the Mainland China population. In 1958 and thereafter, Red China converted hundreds of thousands of "collective farms" into 26,000 Peoples' Communes. A study by SEATO (South Eastern Asia Treaty Organization) shows that this was accompanied by gross regimentation, destruction of the family unit, and widespread forcing of women into manual labor.

22. QUESTION: **What is the prime purpose of the "Commune" system?**

ANSWER: It has several important purposes, including the making of the Chinese peasants into serfs of the State, as Lenin and Stalin did with the Russian peasants in outlining and carrying through the collectivization of the land. Its immediate, and perhaps primary, purpose, however, is to disrupt the family unit by bringing about communal kitchens and extensive kindergartens. In this way the children will be completely divorced from

the influence of their parents and reared under strict Communist indoctrination.

23. QUESTION: **What has been the main aim of the Communists of the world so far as the United
States is concerned, since Red China became a reality?**

ANSWER: In the United States itself, with a climax in
1950, the Communists and their appeaser
friends sought to bring about quick recognition of Red China by the United States and
admission of Red China to the United Nations. It is clear that with the double veto of
Soviet Russia and Red China, plus the intim-
idation and propaganda which have been
carried on by all Soviet-controlled governments, that such action would have captured
the United Nations for the "Soviet bloc,"
imprisoned the United States even more than
it is today as a weak and ineffective member
of the United Nations. Thereby the door
would have been opened quite easily for Soviet conquest of the world.

24. QUESTION: **What halted this well-laid scheme to influence the United States to recognize Red
China in 1950?**

ANSWER: According to Robert Morris, the former
counsel for the Senate Sub-Committee on Internal Security, Earl Browder bitterly stated
to him that the recognition of Red China in
1950 was already pre-arranged. According to
Browder, this recognition was halted by the
testimony of Louis F. Budenz before the
Tydings Committee and then again before
the Senate Sub-Committee on Internal Security, which testimony showed beyond

doubt that there was a widespread scheme to poison the American mind on China.

The second reason for halting the recognition of Red China was the Korean War, which taught the American people how brutally the Chinese Communists carry out their purposes.

As a result, on every occasion since, both houses of the Congress have overwhelmingly voted against any recognition of Red China.

25. QUESTION: **What was a prominent device which the appeasers used after 1950 to try to obtain Red Chinese recognition?**

ANSWER: They set on foot the rumor, absolutely unsubstantiated by any fact, that the Mao Tse-tung regime was about to break with Soviet Russia. It was pictured as becoming "another Tito."

26. QUESTION: **Was there any proof to oppose this rumor?**

ANSWER: This rumor, which appeared in the columns of many of the commentators who are constantly taking the appeaser side, flew in the face of the facts in regard to Red Chinese relations with Soviet Russia. As early as the Seventh World Congress of the Communist International, in 1935, the Chinese Communist Party was of such high standing in the international Communist movement that it was chosen to give the "comradely greeting" to the delegates of all the other Communist parties. On that occasion, it declared: "Long live the world proletarian revolution! Long live our leader and teacher, Comrade Stalin."

This was continually through the years the attitude of the Chinese Communist leadership toward Soviet Russia and its leadership. It has gone down to the present. On June 2, 1959, Soong Ching Ling—the former Madame Sun Yatsen—Vice-premier of Red China, wrote an article in the **Peking Review** for the comrades of the world, entitled "China and the Soviet Forever Stand Together."

27. QUESTION: **How did this important personage, speaking for the Chinese Communist leaders, prove the unity of Red China with Soviet Russia?**

ANSWER: By many arguments which pointed clearly to the leadership of the Soviet Communist Party in the international Communist conspiracy. Above all she stressed: "Joint actions based on mutually arrived-at decisions derived from the common Marxist-Leninist world outlook."

28. QUESTION: **If Red China had proved temporarily to be "another Tito" would that have helped the United States?**

ANSWER: It would not, just as Tito has proved to be the stalking-horse for Moscow. Tito, by pretending to be somewhat different from Moscow, gets money from the United States to bolster his Communist-controlled regime and at the same time does almost everything that Moscow wants in the international arena, voting with Moscow continuously in the United Nations. This was strikingly demonstrated when Red Yugoslavia voted with Soviet Russia against any mild criticism or inquiry into the savage Soviet butchery in

Hungary. That vote for the Butchery of Budapest was registered once again as late as December 12, 1959.

29. QUESTION: **Being foiled by the common sense of the American people concerning the "Titoism" of the Chinese Communist leaders, what have the appeasers in America lately done?**

ANSWER: Ever since the visit of Nikita Khrushchev to this country, the appeasers have a new and equally false argument for dealing with Red China. They have said in newspaper after newspaper that Khrushchev is an angel of peace but that Red China is "interfering with his peace plans."

The argument is that we must find a way to draw near to Red China and curb its belligerency, probably with the aid of Red China's mentor, the new Stalin, Nikita Khrushchev!

30. QUESTION: **Do the policies and principles of Red China itself demonstrate the folly of dealing with that regime by recognition or otherwise?**

ANSWER: They emphatically do. We can give but two instances here but they are fundamental. One of them is Mao Tse-tung's famous political document, **Imperialists and All Reactionaries are Paper Tigers.** This was distributed in many different languages by the Foreign Languages Press of Peking in 1958, for the education of the comrades of the world. Its theme is, repeated over and over again, that the United States can and will eventually be completely destroyed as an independent nation by Red Chinese cooperation with other world Communist forces.

The other instance is furnished by the leading article in the October, 1959, number of the **World Marxist Review,** Moscow's chief directive-giver for the Communists of the world. This article is written by Liu Shao-chi, now "President" of Red China, and is entitled **"The Triumph of Marxism-Leninism in China."** When one studies its many pages, it can be seen that Red China has been chosen by Moscow to be the mentor of the "new revolutions" in Iraq, Cuba, and other mid-Eastern and Latin American nations. These "new revolutions" are being carried on in such a manner that they appear to be non-Communist, thus "exonerating" Khrushchev of having anything to do with them and at the same time being Communist controlled.

31. QUESTION: **What, then, is our proper policy for Red China in order to safeguard the United States and serve freedom?**

ANSWER: There can be only one, which the American people will have to press constantly on their senators and representatives. This is the policy of a firm stand, such as was taken of late years by the late Secretary of State, John Foster Dulles. In 1958, the Chinese Communists attacked Quemoy and Matsu. Immediately, all the voices of appeasement in America were heard declaring that unless we agreed to give up Quemoy and Matsu and even Formosa, great calamities and catastrophies would come down on our heads. This was, for instance, the tenor of letter after letter to the **New York Times.** When Mr. Dulles

refused to budge and refused to betray freedom in Formosa, there was no war and there
was no calamity.

SUGGESTED READINGS

Chiang Kai-shek, **Soviet Russia in China**, Farrar, Straus and
Cudahy, N.Y.

Chamberlin, William Henry, **America's Second Crusade,**
Henry Regnery, Chicago.

McCarthy, Senator Joseph R., **America's Retreat from Victory,** Devin Adair, N.Y.

Monsterleet, Jean, S. J., **Out of the Orient Valor, Account of
the Martyrs in China,** Henry Regnery, Chicago.

Walker, Richard L., **China Under Communism, The First
Five Years,** Yale University Press, New Haven, Conn.

SEATO, Southeast Asia Treaty Organization, **Life in the
Communes,** a study taken from analysis of the Red Chinese
press, published in Bangkok, Thailand.

ALSO FOR POSSIBLE AUXILIARY READING

Draskovich, Slobodan M., **Tito, Moscow's Trojan Horse,**
Regnery, Chicago.

DeJaegher, Raymond J., written with Irene Corbally Kuhn,
The Enemy Within, Doubleday, N.Y.

Sih, Paul K., **Decision for China, Communism or Christianity,** Regnery, Chicago.

Tennien, Mark, Rev., **No Secret is Safe,** Farrar, Straus, and
Cudahy, N.Y.

VERY VALUABLE ARE the reports and hearings of the
Senate Sub-Committee on Internal Security, Senate Office
Building, Washington, D.C., particularly those on the Institute of Pacific Relations. Consultation could be also had
with House Committee on Un-American Activities, House
Office Building, Washington, D.C., on testimony of Protestant missionaries.

CHAPTER XII

THE DEFEAT OF COMMUNISM

1. QUESTION: **Are there any effective ways, short of war, to check the international Communist conspirracy?**

   ANSWER: Yes. But in order to do this, courage, persistence, and intelligent knowledge of our foe are required. At least these attributes are necessary on the part of community leaders. If we proceed in this task with humble faith in God, we shall be greatly strengthened in this effort.

2. QUESTION: **Is it so difficult for intelligent Americans to master a knowledge of atheistic Communism—its nature, its line at any particular period, and its true attitude toward reforms?**

   ANSWER: This is not at all difficult for those who are obliged to take biology, physics, higher mathematics, philosophy, and other difficult subjects as early as high school. We must recognize that there has been a mental block created on this subject by what Pope Pius XI has called "the conspiracy of silence" on the part of most of the general press of the world concerning the true character of Communism and its techniques.

3. QUESTION: **What would be the first step to be taken in the battle against Communism?**

ANSWER: Obviously, since we are combating what is at its core militant atheism, our first step must be to affirm to ourselves and others our belief in God. The recitation of the phrase, "I believe in God, the Father Almighty, Creator of heaven and earth" must not only be on our lips but also inspire our activities.

4. QUESTION: **What must we then do in order to help save America from complete defeat?**

ANSWER: We can profit by the 1959 message of the Catholic Bishops on "freedom and peace," and understand and make others understand that appeasement will never bring peace. It always brings war or slavery or both. For the past twenty-five years, we can point out, the United States has been by and large pursuing a policy of abject appeasement before Soviet Russia—too much of our press, our television, radio, magazines, and too many of our government officials doing eventually or championing eventually what Moscow wanted us to do or to champion. In other words, the Kremlin has too often dominated the American mind through the Communist line. If we are to save our country, it is clear we must halt this process, which came to a new high point for Soviet Power with the invitation to Nikita Khrushchev to visit the United States in 1959.

5. QUESTION: **What must we understand, first of all, and make others understand in order to protect America at the present hour?**

ANSWER: As is evident from our studies and conclusions in previous chapters, we must first of all understand the nature of Communism and make others understand it. This is the

THE DEFEAT OF COMMUNISM

great weakness of the United States today, that many of its officials, editors, and educators live in total darkness as to the true nature of this enemy of religion and freedom. The basic world outlook of Communism, we have seen, is dialectical materialism, which makes the Kremlin and its allies determined to conquer the world.

6. QUESTION: **Will the Kremlin use both fair means and foul to accomplish this world conquest purpose?**

ANSWER: That is precisely what we have proved in our previous considerations, from Marxist-Leninist morality, which states that any method must be used to forward the Communist cause. This makes it practically impossible for us to engage in cultural exchanges, summit conferences, and the other methods of "peaceful coexistence" which the Kremlin so far has most skillfully advocated to our own detriment.

7. QUESTION: **What can we show has been the result of our yielding during the past twenty-five years to the wishes of the Kremlin as represented by the Communist line?**

ANSWER: It has led to the constant shrinking of the free world and the growth of Soviet Power with our acquiescence and assistance.

8. QUESTION: **Have there been good examples of what Americans can do to take a stand against our Government's agreeing with the Communist line?**

ANSWER: There have been a number, including classes in the Principles and Techniques of Communism given in many cities throughout the country. These classes have examined Communism analytically and critically, as a scientist would examine a poison in order to offset its evil effects.

9. QUESTION: **Can you give an example of how ignorance of the Communist line has prevented certain patriotic Americans from defending this country against Communist aggression?**

ANSWER: This is strikingly illustrated by the whole course of Khrushchev's recent tactics for the belittling and serious harassing of the United States. By our permitting his visit here, our Government has opened the door for his appearing as an angel of peace, while at the same time he has forwarded in Iraq, Cuba, and other Latin American and Mid-Eastern countries "new revolutions" and violent demonstrations against the United States. These appear to be "non-Communist" though controlled and directed by Communists behind the scenes. This is revealed by the discussions in the **World Marxist Review** championing these "new revolutions," the **Iraqi Review,** the comments in **Political Affairs** and **The Worker** on Cuba, and the resolutions of the Seventeenth National Convention of the Communist Party of the United States.

This latter convention was held in New York City on December 10-13, 1959, and among other moves echoing Moscow's wishes declared for militant support "to the Cuban, Iraqi, and other revolutions." These were the "marching orders" given to the convention in advance by its leader, William Z. Foster, in the December, 1959, issue of **Political Affairs.**

10. QUESTION: **From the study of Communist documents, what do we learn about the pitfalls we should avoid because the Communists want us to fall into them?**

ANSWER: It is clear that nothing could be more fatal to the battle against Communism than in confusing anti-Semitism, anti-Negroism, and anti-Unionism with anti-Communism. The Catholic Bishops in their statement of 1959 wisely reminded us of this by pointing to the other problems, requiring reforms, which confront the United States.

Probably the greatest pitfall is ignorance of the nature, goals and methods of Communism. We should also add prejudice, bigotry and ignorance of America and her history.

11. QUESTION: **Would it also be a mistake to charge everyone who forwards the Communist line with being a Communist?**

ANSWER: That would be a serious mistake. The very essence of Communism, as we have seen, is to use non-Communists to forward the Communist line. In the United States today it is non-Communist editors, educators, and the like who in considerable measure are advancing the wishes of Moscow, stimulated to do so by the concealed Communists.

12. QUESTION: **Can Americans—armed with a knowledge of the nature of Communism, the contents of the Communist line and the Communist attitude toward reforms—achieve anything by exercising their rights of citizenship and**

getting in touch with their Senators and Representatives on this subject?

ANSWER: They can be particularly effective in the defense of the United States in doing just that, letting Senators and Representatives know what is the Communist line at any particular period. The Communists, in the pages of **The Worker** and otherwise, are being urged constantly to deluge Congress with letters favorable to that line. This is one of the secrets of Soviet success in the United States.

13. QUESTION: **Can we say that prayer is essential to achievement in the battle against atheistic Communism?**

ANSWER: Since Communism is "a satanic scourge" and does carry forward "diabolical propaganda," as Pius XI has so well said, prayer becomes an essential in the battle against slavery and tyranny which it brings. There is hope that by prayer we may even be able to offset the atheistic education now so widespread in Soviet Russia and in all other Marxist-controlled countries.

Father Leopold Braun, who for many years served as American Catholic priest in Moscow, has said that in 1937 to 1939, Soviet Russia conducted a census on those who held religious beliefs. It was so overwhelmingly pro-religious at that time, that the Government has never attempted another such enterprise since; it was too rebuking to the dictatorship and its atheistic propaganda. Prayer will also give us strength and perseverance to proceed intelligently in those duties of citizenship which the present crisis requires and which can lead, with God's help, to final victory over atheistic Communism.

In the history of the Catholic Church, many foes have appeared at different periods who have seemed to threaten truth and religion. If those could be overcome, so today, by prayer, personal sanctity and intelligent application to the present task, Communism can be defeated.

SUPPLEMENT
COMMUNIST WRITINGS CONSULTED

It must be borne in mind that Communist books and documents should not be read by those who are unable to comprehend their true nature. Many of the drugs beneficial to our health are poisons which we would not take without a physician's prescription. Nor would we allow poisons which are injurious to us to lie around the shelves of our homes. And we must recognize that the teachings of Communism constitute intellectual and spiritual poison. If properly forewarned and properly directed in their study, examining them analytically and critically, we shall be able to combat Communism intelligently.

In that spirit, and in order to indicate that these Questions and Answers have been based on Marxist-Leninist documents, out of the "mouth of the enemy" himself, we wish briefly to cite the Communist works which have been consulted for this little study.

They are:

1. The writings of Karl Marx and Frederick Engels from **The Holy Family**, their first publication which proclaimed their atheism, over to **Ludwig Feuerbach** and the **Dialectics of Nature**, by Frederick Engels, which summarized this atheism.

2. The writings of V. I. Lenin, including his **Selected Works,** and comprising such "classics" as his writings against God, his **Imperialism and State and Revolution** (which seeks to demonstrate the necessity of the violent overthrow of the United States and other non-Soviet Governments) and such works as **What Is To Be Done?**

which outlined the character and course of the Communist Party.

3. The writings of Joseph Stalin, Nikita Khrushchev, and Mao Tse-tung—especially **Foundations of Leninism** and **Problems of Leninism** by the first named.

4. Past and current issues of the directive organs of the Communist international conspiracy, which give the line—including the **World Marxist Review,** the **New Times** and **International Affairs** from Moscow, **Political Affairs,** theoretical organ of the Communist Party of the United States, **Marxism Today,** theoretical organ of the Communist Party of Great Britain, and **The Worker,** which has been designated in testimony before Congressional committees aptly as "the telegraph agency of directives to the rank and file members of the conspiracy in this country."

MISCELLANEOUS QUESTIONS
ASKED BY THE YOUTH
DURING MY CONFERENCES AND LECTURES

1. QUESTION: **Are there such things as Communist professional clubs or cells?**

   ANSWER: Yes, cells are standard Communist procedures. Witnesses have testified to a number of people organized by cells in the field of literature, entertainment, education and other professions serving as active Communists.

2. QUESTION: **How would these people be able to influence others?**

   ANSWER: Their acceptance as responsible and intelligent people in the community would give them access to persons and things that would be helpful to the Communist cause or line.

3. QUESTION: **How can intelligent people believe something that denies God and freedom?**

   ANSWER: The idealism which these people erroneously place in Communism brings out a dedication to a cause which gives nothing and demands everything.

4. QUESTION: **Have the liberties of Communists been controlled in America?**

   ANSWER: Records show that the rights of Communists are protected by law in our country better than nearly anywhere else in the world today.

5. QUESTION: **Why so many Communists?**

    ANSWER: The millions of modern pagans, with little or no belief in God, provide a ripe field for Communist conversion. The unemployed, the homeless, and the hungry are attracted to this system hoping for better living conditions. The intellectuals identified with the movement, and there are many, see in Communism the good society or they accept it as a natural consequence of their materialistic education.

6. QUESTION: **Why has it spread?**

    ANSWER: Too few have been able to understand its nature and therefore fall victim to the deceit concealed by its promises. In some countries under the tyranny of Moscow millions have been educated since childhood to learn and become dedicated to Communism. Furthermore, every Communist is a missionary for the cause.

7. QUESTION: **What is the Communist attitude toward truth?**

    ANSWER: If questioned, they would swear in court on a stack of Bibles that they were never members of the Communist Party and would deny any charges made against them. Recall those who have taken refuge behind the Fifth Amendment.

8. QUESTION: **Is it possible for a country like ours to exist side by side with Russia?**

    ANSWER: Lenin said, "It is unreasonable that the Soviet Republic should continue to exist for a long period side by side with capitalist states. Ultimately one or the other must conquer." Unless Communism changes it is difficult to see how any country can coexist with it. World conquest is its goal.

9. QUESTION: **Is Communism a social theory?**

   ANSWER: It is not only a false economic, political and social theory but also an entire way of life which controls thought as well as action.

10. QUESTION: **Does Communism feel that Christianity is a real enemy?**

    ANSWER: Lenin felt that, "One day Communism and Christianity will have to stand face to face in single combat."

11. QUESTION: **Does talk of material gains serve Communist purposes?**

    ANSWER: Yes. If our strength and concern lies only in the area of economics then Communism, which explains all things by economics, finds friends in those who are always concerned with the problem.

12. QUESTION: **Is it possible that Communists may pose as religious people?**

    ANSWER: Yes. Communism would use any means at its disposal to convert, and the organization of religion offers them an avenue perhaps as rich as many others.

13. QUESTION: **Are Communists interested in the rights of minorities?**

    ANSWER: They are only interested in using them to achieve their own final victory, not in the solving of the many problems of these groups.

14. QUESTION: **How should Catholics resist Communism?**

    ANSWER: Spiritual and moral resistance, constant study

of its techniques, knowledge and resistance to its methods are needed to answer and overcome Communism.

15. QUESTION: **What type of man is the Communist man?**

ANSWER: A Communist is asked to display discipline and hardening in the struggle against the enemy as well as in opposition to anything deviating from the Communist line. He should combine the knowledge of what he must do with the will power to carry it through. (Browder—**Build the United People's Front**)

16. QUESTION: **Why do Communists call religion the opium of the people?**

ANSWER: Opium has a deadening effect which is what Communists feel religion has in the life of man. Say the Communists:—

1. It teaches the rich their rights, thereby recognizing the exploitation of the poor.
2. It teaches the poor their duties towards the rich ruling class.
3. It instills a passive spirit among the masses which destroys any desire on their part for bettering their conditions.

Actually, these same arguments can be turned against Communism itself.

17. QUESTION: **Is high income a guarantee against Communism?**

ANSWER: No. There are perhaps more Communists among the higher income groups in our big cities than in Tobacco Road.

18. QUESTION: **Do Communists easily spot people who might sympathize with their cause?**

ANSWER: In groups and organizations, companies and

industries, well-trained Communists have their eyes and ears open to enlist possible followers.

19. QUESTION: **Was Russia always the prime target of the Communists?**

ANSWER: No. Karl Marx thought that Russia would be one of the last countries to adopt Communism.

20. QUESTION: **Is it true that Russia under Communism is as far advanced after 40 years as America is after 150?**

ANSWER: From all the available evidence this is not true. Communism, however, has brushed almost one third of the human family behind the iron or bamboo curtains. The real battle of the present and especially of the future is for the minds of men. Spiritual armor is still our greatest need.

21. QUESTION: **What do Americans need to know about Communism?**

ANSWER: Because of the widespread ignorance and confusion among the American people concerning the nature of Communism, it is important that they learn the tactics and purposes of this movement. Because of their indifference towards this evil force they could become easy prey for this vicious enemy.

22. QUESTION: **How would one spot a Communist-front organization?**

ANSWER: If the literature published follows the Communist line or is printed by the Communist press, or the organization continuously receives favorable mention in the Communist publications, it is likely that the organization is under strong Communist influence.

ADDITIONAL QUESTIONS ASKED BY STUDENTS OF JOURNALISM

1. QUESTION: **What is the attitude of the Communists towards the press?**

   ANSWER: They disarm the people by suppressing all unfavorable news so that they will know nothing except what they wish them to know.

2. QUESTION: **How important do Communists consider communications?**

   ANSWER: Communists feel it is necessary to isolate power by seizure of communication posts, telephones, telegraphs, radio transport and other means of contact.

3. QUESTION: **What has the Communist press said about the Church?**

   ANSWER: It feels that a concentration of all the evil forces in the world is found in the Vatican. (Pravada—March, 1947.)

4. QUESTION: **What part of the newspaper business would Communists be interested in serving?**

   ANSWER: They strive to exert much influence in an editorial or writing capacity, in slanting news items for propaganda and by falsifying facts.

5. QUESTION: **Does this mean they would write editorials?**

   ANSWER: Not necessarily, but they might be called in on editorial conferences where they would exert their influence. With their use of the press and their publication of their own papers, magazines and books, they penetrate practically every country.

6. QUESTION: **How could they promote their ideas in a free press?**

ANSWER: The guarantees they enjoy make it possible to spread their ideas with greater ease in the American press, even if done more subtly by placing emphasis on what is called the Communist line.

7. QUESTION: **In what capacity would they best serve their purposes in the theater world?**

ANSWER: As playwrights, producers, directors and actors.

8. QUESTION: **How could these people sell Communism if millions of Americans were against it?**

ANSWER: By their presence in an industry of ideas. This is extremely important to the promotion of Communism. Surely, the mass-communication field is a rich one for selling Communism and fooling a people who are content with material possessions.

9. QUESTION: **Are any Communists in the film and stage industry?**

ANSWER: There seems to be many. Numbers would be hard to determine. There might be a few who could be proved as active members of a Communist cell. But sympathy with the cause could make of these highly placed people a ready tool for Communist ideas and promotion.

10. QUESTION: **How may these Communist influences best be offset?**

    ANSWER: By large numbers of dedicated young religious and loyal Americans entering into the vital fields of communication.

11. QUESTION: **Is radio and TV a good place for the spread of Communism?**

    ANSWER: Yes. The large numbers of teenagers and adults who determine what is heard and seen can be the means of promoting some of the star performers whose ideas are alien to the best traditions of this country.

12. QUESTION: **Would Communists prefer to sabotage communications or to use them?**

    ANSWER: At the present time they can gain more by encouraging young intellectuals, sympathetic to Communism, writers, technicians, actors and others to get into the field of communications rather than to destroy the existing institutions.

13. QUESTION: **Is the extreme modern form of art Communistic?**

    ANSWER: Nothing could be farther from the truth. The only kinds of art—painting, sculpture, music and writing—tolerated by the rulers of Soviet Russia and other Communist nations are those in the most traditional forms; paintings in a realistic style that most American artists have left behind, music that sounds conservative compared to more advanced American compositions, etc. All the arts are subjected to propaganda purposes, with little or no opportunity for self-expression.

This does not mean that modern artists have no sympathy for Communism. Some of them have given definite signs of attachment to Communist ideas; but the chances are that they would be miserable if they were living in the Soviet Union.

14. QUESTION: **Can the press propagate the Communist line without being detected?**

    ANSWER: The most effective way to promote the Communist idea is by doing so in a subtle fashion that does not betray itself. Openly Communist newspapers and magazines are easily discredited; those secretly Communist deceive many.

15. QUESTION: **Who in a newspaper would be most influential in handing out the Communist line without detection?**

    ANSWER: Many aspects of newspaper and magazine work allow opportunity for infiltration of ideas which could be subversive.

    1. Editorial writers: Here it is very possible to confuse issues or present material that distorts the true meaning of events.

    2. Editors: The selection of news and the prominence given certain stories, as well as the suppression of others, can slant the meaning behind events. Moreover, it is possible to give certain stories to those writers who are sympathetic to the Communist line who will interpret the matter accordingly.

    3. Reporters: In actually covering a story it is possible to give several interpretations

to the facts; it is also possible to select and suppress quotations in a deceptive manner. By controlling the source of a story, reporters can follow the Communist line rather than the true facts as they are.

4. Pressmen and distributors: By strikes and the threat of strikes it is possible to severely handicap newspapers and cause immense losses of funds. Communists like to infiltrate unions which distribute and print papers because this gives them influence and power.

16. QUESTION: **How can one detect a newpaper that follows the Communist line?**

ANSWER: This is not an easy task. One test would be to note that the paper refrains always from condemning Communism and Communists. Another test would be to watch the issues involving Communism and the free world and see with what solicitude the paper follows the Communist interests.

17. QUESTION: **What is the danger in being soft on Communism?**

ANSWER: The danger here is that such an attitude allows the evil to flourish undetected and without fear of exposure until grave damage has been done to society.

18. QUESTION: **Why would newsmen, with so much experience, follow the Communist line?**

ANSWER: Newsmen of long experience are seldom impressed by Communist tactics, but occasionally men are planted on papers for the express purpose of influencing the news and slanting its presentation.

19. QUESTION: **What should one do when he suspects a newspaper is Communist influenced?**

ANSWER: Such a paper should be studied carefully to be sure of its character and then exposed by competent authorities in order to protect the public.

20. QUESTION: **Are all Communists alike? Are Socialists, radicals and pacifists just about the same as Communists?**

ANSWER: No. The word "Communist" can refer to a variety of beliefs almost as bewildering as the contemporary use of the word "Christian." The belief that all Communists are devoted to achieving precisely the same objectives in precisely the same way is as absurd as the belief that there are no points of personal disagreement among people in the free world. According to the best information available, there are deep and bitter disagreements among the leaders of Soviet Russia—a fact which, if properly exploited, could give the free world enormous strategic advantages. The fact remains, however, that a clearly-defined "party line" exists, and that (at least in public) dedicated Communists give strong lip-service to official policy.

On the second point, it is impossible to stress too plainly the necessity of keeping in mind clear distinctions between Communists and non-Communists, whatever the ideological hue of the latter may be. We should not indulge in the practice of branding as Communists those who hold unpopular ideas.

21. QUESTION: **In a general way how should we oppose Communism?**

ANSWER: 1. Above all else, we should pray for the Communists, that they may be converted to the truth. Catholic prayers for the conversion of Russia have been prescribed for recitation at the end of low Masses for many years.

2. Since the spread of Communism is largely a result of our own evil ways, we should make all possible efforts to amend our own lives and those of others around us. A world in which all Christians lived up to the obligations of their religion would be a world in which Communism would disappear.

3. Communism thrives in an atmosphere of materialism. To combat Communism, we must place the things of the spirit foremost in our lives and bring them often to the attention of others.

4. Social injustice feeds Communism. We should work to eliminate such things as racial hatred, economic exploitation, degrading living conditions and irresponsibility in positions of power.

5. Communism works through ignorance and lies. It can be fought with truth.

6. Communism is a political threat. We should not vote for a Communist or for a person who collaborates with Communists. This does not mean that we are obliged to support a particular politician simply

because of his avowed or actual opposition to Communism.

7. Communism is a military threat. We should be ready to oppose it, even to give our lives if necessary, in the event of actual war.

22. QUESTION: **What do you specifically recommend for the American youth in respect to their opposition to the Communist peril?**

ANSWER: Be vigilant, informed, and live within the laws of God and the country.

Be studious, and give the maximum time to your education.

Be concerned about the higher things of life, especially the love of God and one another.

Be poor in spirit, avoiding the false and fatal standards of our age of materialism.

Be holy and strive for the heights of personal sanctity. Our times need scholars who are saints and saints who are scholars.

Be loyal Americans and represent the best and not the worst in American life.

Communism in our time has concentrated its hostility on the United States as the most powerful of the nations not yet under its sway.

What the future will bring when you reach adult life depends on what we all do in the present. We are under attack in many ways by an enemy whose basic will is to destroy the order of life in our country in order to make room for Communism.

If we live as a nation under God, praying as if everything depended on God and working as if everything depended on ourselves, we shall maintain this blessed country of ours as a citadel of freedom, a light for the world and a source of undying hope for millions of enslaved peoples.

God Bless America!

DAUGHTERS OF ST. PAUL

Missionary Sisters of the Catholic Editions

50 St. Paul's Ave.
BOSTON 30, MASS.

315 Washington Street
BOSTON 8, MASS.

381 Dorchester Street
SO. BOSTON 27, MASS.

78 Fort Place
STATEN ISLAND 1, N. Y.

325 Main Street
FITCHBURG, MASS.

39 Erie Street
BUFFALO 2, N. Y.

141 West Rayen Ave.
YOUNGSTOWN 3, OHIO

114 East Main Plaza
SAN ANTONIO 5, TEXAS

827 Fifth Ave.
SAN DIEGO 1, CALIF.

86 Bolton Ave.
ALEXANDRIA, LA.

2700 Biscayne Blvd.
MIAMI, FLORIDA

33 West Notre Dame
MONTREAL, CAN.

134 Westmount Ave.
TORONTO, CAN.